Oma

Strategic
Marketing

Published by Amazon (London, United Kingdom)

ISBN: 9798625632492

TABLE OF CONTENTS

4

Introduction

1 OVERVIEW

Strategy and marketing go hand in hand. Strategy refers to the overriding direction that determines the planning path for an organisation, given its assets and capabilities, its values, and the external business environment (i.e., its market, competition, customers, etc.). The strategy determines the firm's objectives, plans and tactics.

In the past, marketing was largely relegated to a tactical role, which means that it was mainly seen as a demand-stimulating support function concerned with the day-to-day management of the market (e.g., advertising, sales promotion, channel management). While some people still see it that way, nowadays the most forward-thinking organisations have realised that the role of marketing should be elevated to a strategic level.

Today's fast-changing environment increasingly emphasises the corporate need for market responsiveness, customer focus, service orientation, and the like. These are all core marketing activities. Thus, marketing should have significant input into higher-level strategy to read and shape market dynamics. Strategy development needs to happen at the business unit level and be driven by the market and the external environment, rather than merely by internal considerations. Market management needs to be proactive and future-oriented in order to capitalise on opportunities and to deal with the rapid rate of change in the external environment. As the key boundary-spanning function of an organisation, marketing can be critical to strategy development and execution.

In this book, we are going to adopt a strategic approach to marketing. The underlying process is detailed in Figure 1, which constitutes the basic structure of the book. This book aims to summarise fundamental concepts in strategic marketing in a concise way, by drawing on important research (both well-established work and the latest research in the field), and leading sources (references and extra readings are provided at the end of each section).

The book begins with Part 1. Before an organisation can implement a marketing strategy, people within it must have a clear understanding of the role that marketing should play within the firm, how it should be organised, the kind of culture necessary to achieve a competitive advantage, and how financial value is generated through marketing activities. These topics are the subject of Part 1.

Figure 1: Overview of the strategic marketing process

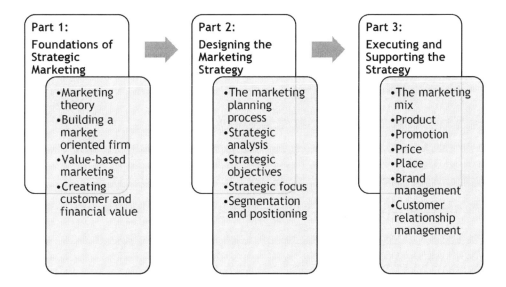

Part 2 focuses on how a marketing strategy can be designed. It is essential to have a planning process that is systematic and ongoing. Everything starts with strategic analysis, where managers carefully assess key external and internal factors, focusing primarily on the customers, the competitors, the market and the environment in which the firm competes. Once that is done, the firm is able to determine its strategic objective and focus; these are essentially the means through which the organisation aims to achieve its goals. Next, the business needs to be clear about its target market and the positioning of its products and services within that market.

Finally, management needs to ensure that the strategy is properly executed and supported by marketing tactics, which are the subject of Part 3. This requires the management of the marketing mix, often referred to as the 4 Ps of marketing (product, promotion, price and place). Companies are also realising that one of their most crucial assets is their brand. The brand can go above and beyond the product or service itself in differentiating the company's offerings in the mind of its customers and can even account for much of a company's market value. Therefore, strategic brand management is also discussed. Finally, marketing is about creating enduring customer value in the long term. For this reason, Part 3 closes with a discussion of customer relationship management, as it has increasingly become the cornerstone of marketing strategy efforts within many leading organisations.

Part I: Foundations of Strategic Marketing

2 INTRODUCTION TO MARKETING THEORY

2.1 WHAT IS MARKETING?

When asked to define "marketing", many people, including many business managers, may suggest that it means "advertising" or "selling". While marketing does encompass these activities, it is much more than just advertising, selling, or catchy slogans, particularly when implemented at a strategic level.

Marketing theory was developed by borrowing extensively from other disciplines. Indeed, the assumptions of marketing theory can be traced back to the 17th and 18th century doctrine of economic liberalism. In 1776, Adam Smith argued that the process of exchange is driven by individual needs. Smith's view was that the greatest wealth for both individuals and society would be brought about by individuals being left free to advance their own interests. In this system, competition acts as a protective mechanism to regulate the economy (e.g., by lowering prices to a natural level). This is the foundation of exchange theory: people have a propensity to exchange one thing for another and are therefore dependent on one another. The process of exchange is therefore driven by individual wants and needs. However, while economists have long argued that consumer needs should be the starting point for business thinking, the question remained as to how to translate that into practice. And this is where marketing came in (Elliott, 2000; Chadwick-Jones, 1976).

Marketing provides necessary direction for production (and other functions within an organisation) and helps to ensure that appropriate goods and services are produced and made available to customers. In essence, it is concerned with what customers need or want, and should guide what is produced and offered to them. Marketing begins with potential customer needs, not with the production process. Marketing is about anticipating needs and determining what products are to be developed. This includes factors such as product design and packaging, prices or fees, use of intermediaries, transportation and storage, advertising and customer service.

In a sense, the aim of marketing is to identify customers' needs and meet those needs so well that the product almost sells itself. So, there can be very effective marketing without much persuasion at all!

Marketing may be formally defined as the performance of activities that seek to achieve an organisation's objectives by anticipating customers' needs and directing a flow of need-satisfying goods and services from producer to customer. A company implements the marketing concept when it aims all of its efforts, in a coordinated and integrated manner, at simultaneously satisfying its customers' needs and achieving its own corporate goals (see below, the Marketing company era).

2.2 THE "EVOLUTION" OF MARKETING

Figure 2: The "evolution" of marketing

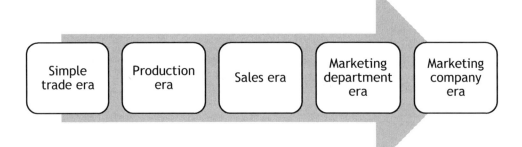

Studies of how marketing evolved over time within organisations have found that there are at least five distinct stages of marketing's "evolution". It should be noted that the term "evolution" is employed rather loosely here, to indicate that the application of marketing theory has evolved or changed over time. However, it does not necessarily mean that all contemporary organisations have adopted an application of marketing that is consistent with the latest incarnation of marketing thinking. In fact, some companies are still employing antiquated approaches to marketing management. Some organisations are still very product-driven, for example: they come up with good products and then try to find a market for them. Yet, it is in the interest of businesses to adapt to the "evolution" of marketing, by ensuring that the best approach is adopted. The five stages of marketing's "evolution" are depicted in Figure 2.

The Simple Trade Era

Before the Industrial Revolution, people produced what they then consumed. In this environment, commonly referred to as the pure subsistence economy, anything in excess was sold or traded within the town. In this pure subsistence economy, marketing was redundant, as each household made what they later consumed. Later on, with the rise of the Industrial Revolution, companies started to produce the goods that people consumed. As the producers and the consumers of the products were not the same entities anymore, there was a rising need for exchanges.

The Production Era

In the production era many companies' main priority was the reduction of the costs of production. Businesses believed that exchanges could be enhanced by lowering the costs of production, which, in turn, created the ability to pass along the cost saving to customers and decrease prices. This focus on production (which lasted until the 1920s) was fuelled by such milestones as Henry Ford's invention of the assembly line and the more efficient work principles advanced by Fredrick Taylor's scientific management movement. As a result of these modernisations, managers realised that mass production can reduce unit costs of production and increased profit possibilities.

The Sales Era

In the sales era, businesses' main priority was to sell their products, through various techniques. Companies, as a result of the economic climate of the time, realised that to enhance the sales of their products, they can use promotional techniques that inform customers about the product and/or persuade customers to purchase from them. These firms were not necessarily concerned with satisfying the customer, but rather with selling the product. The sales era dictated the business environment through the 1930s until World War II, when companies' production facilities were adjusted to building machinery for the war.

The Marketing Department Era

From about the 1950s, firms realised that they needed a set of criteria to determine which products would be manufactured and which would not, as well as a new management function that would integrate many related activities, such as advertising, sales and procurement into a single section of the organisation: the marketing department. It was also at this time that many firms realised that the company's purpose was no longer to manufacture a variety of products, but to satisfy their customers. The change in company thinking or purpose from that of manufacturing products to that of satisfying customers was truly revolutionary and had many implications. Firms that see themselves as manufacturers of products use selling techniques that are preoccupied with converting products into cash. On the other hand, companies that consider themselves as marketers concentrate on meeting the needs of their customers through their product development, delivery and consumption experience. As the sales function centres around the needs of the seller, marketing concentrates on the needs of the buyer. The marketing era saw businesses shifting their focus from manufacturing the product to meeting customer needs. Companies with a customer orientation aim to manufacture products that will satisfy customer needs and induce buying behaviour.

The Marketing Company Era

Beginning in the 1960s some firms had implemented a customer-oriented philosophy to the point where the marketing department set the agenda for the entire company. These types of firms are referred to as marketing companies: they are firms that have moved from simply having a marketing department that follows a customer orientation to having marketing principles guide the company's direction. In marketing companies, marketing sets company operating policy, including technical research, procurement, production, advertising, and sales. In these firms marketing is the basic motivating force for all activities within the corporation, from finance to sales to production, with the objective of satisfying the needs of the customer. Successful companies today tend to be those that embrace this marketing company orientation. Simply put, it's risky when your marketing is stuck in a different "era".

General Electric was among the first to express the view that marketing should be central to all the organisation's activities. In 1952, their annual report read:

> *"Our philosophy introduces the marketing man [sic] at the beginning rather than the end of the production cycle and would integrate marketing into each phase of the business. Thus marketing will establish for the engineer, the designer and the manufacturing man what the customer*

wants in a given product, what price he is willing to pay, and where and when it is wanted."

This statement was met with some scepticism within GE. Particularly by R&D people, product designers and the like, who often viewed marketing merely as a demand-stimulation support function. But GE's statement did not mean to imply that marketers always know best! It simply argued that the company should try and start with marketing, rather than end with it. That is, GE's philosophy was that everything should begin with a close understanding of the external environment (e.g., customer needs, market trends, competing alternatives) and that marketing is entrusted with bringing all that information into the company. In other words, marketing acts as a window between the organisation and the external environment. Once that information is brought in, assimilated and acted upon by all functions, the likelihood of market success is higher, and the company does not have to try and convince customers to buy something they do not need. Everything becomes a lot more effective and efficient.

This was the start of a new managerial philosophy which two years later was labelled "the marketing concept" by management scholar Peter Drucker. Businesses that bring departments together with the aim to meet customer needs are following the marketing concept. The marketing concept states that if all of the organisation's functions are focused on customer needs, profits can be achieved by satisfying those needs. Customer needs can be met by enhanced customer service, product or pricing adjustments as well as distribution changes, with attention to long-term profits. Profit is still an important and legitimate objective and a marketing company does not seek to satisfy customers' needs at any cost.

In short, the marketing concept is based on 3 factors:

1. Customer satisfaction.
2. A total company effort, or integration.
3. Profit, not just sales, as a company's objective.

Customer satisfaction is about giving customers what they need. The idea is that customers are the core of the company's operations and that everything starts with customer needs. Integration involves departments and people cooperating. Each department needs to see itself as a part of a coordinated system aimed at satisfying customers. Everyone within the organisation is guided by the needs of customers and not by the preferences of individual departments; all managers and their departments should work together because the output of one business area may be the input to another. Finally, the corporate goal should be a balance between costs involved in satisfying customers and how much customers will contribute to the business. Corporate objectives and customer satisfaction need to be balanced – thus, the implication is that not all customers may be valuable.

2.3 MARKET ORIENTATION

How should these ideas be translated into practice? The marketing concept is a business philosophy, an ideal, or a policy statement. Over the years, marketing scholars and practitioners alike have been looking for guidelines as to how the marketing concept should be implemented. The result of these efforts is the concept of "market orientation".

Market orientation is the implementation of the marketing concept philosophy, or how the marketing concept translates into actual activities and behaviours within the organisation. In short, a market-oriented organisation is one whose actions are consistent with the marketing concept.

There are several alternative views on what a market orientation constitutes exactly and how it should be implemented. One of the dominant views argues that market orientation entails three processes: (1) intelligence generation, (2) intelligence dissemination, and (3) responsiveness to intelligence:

1. *Intelligence generation* involves tapping systematically and continuously into the market, to generate strategically useful information about customers, competitors and collaborators. There are different means through which this can be achieved, including, for instance, secondary sources, such as databases and records, commissioning of market research (e.g., of intermediaries and consumers), and benchmarking and competitive intelligence (e.g., reverse engineering). Another method for generating market intelligence that is proving to be very effective is ethnographic market research, which is discussed later in this book.

2. *Intelligence dissemination* is about sharing the information gathered in the intelligence generation stage. The information that has been generated has no value unless the business does something with it – sharing it in an ongoing and systematic way. It is

important that the organisation develops interfunctional coordination, as it is required to spread strategically important information throughout the organisation (effective flow of information is needed). Examples of ways in which organisations can spread intelligence throughout the firm include cross functional teams, job rotation, internal reporting and documentation or internal marketing. Anything that helps connect people within the organisation, whether formally or informally, can help intelligence dissemination. The crucial point is that like intelligence generation, these are not one-off activities. They must take place continuously in the background.

3. Finally, the organisation needs to *respond to market intelligence* promptly and accurately. This might mean considering whether to match a competitor's price cut or launching a new promotional campaign in response to changing customer preferences. Responding to market intelligence does not necessarily mean that a company needs to react to everything that happens in the external environment. It might simply mean that the relevant information is considered and its potential impact on the business strategy assessed carefully. Then an action may or may not ensue; a company may choose not to do anything after having analysed the intelligence generated. The most important thing is that there are processes in place to deal with the market intelligence that has been generated and disseminated.

To sum up, a company is market oriented when it develops activities and processes that are designed to generate information from the external environment constantly, disseminate that information effectively, and respond to it promptly. Obviously this may be fairly easy for, say, a B2B start-up consisting of its founder and a handful of collaborators; these people know the market well, probably know every single customer by their first name, and they tend to talk a lot to each other because they work in a small and cohesive team. Compare that to a large FMCG multinational with many layers between employees, multiple offices, large departments, and lots of bureaucracy. For the latter company, market orientation may be more difficult to implement.

So, what are the rewards that a company can reap from becoming market oriented? Research has focused on several outcomes, and there is some agreement that irrespective of the context (e.g., services vs tangible goods, turbulent vs non-turbulent markets, country to country differences, B2B vs B2C) companies that are market oriented (and which therefore excel at intelligence generation, dissemination and responsiveness) benefit from: (1) improved organisational performance, (2) better customer consequences, (3) more successful innovation, and (4) positive employee outcomes. Figure 3 summarises the results of some of the research on the benefits of market orientation.

Figure 3: Why is a market orientation desirable?

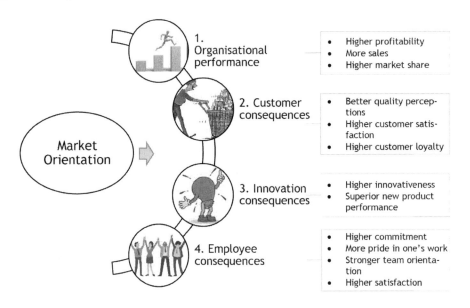

To sum up, businesses that implement a market orientation enjoy improved business performance, have a more satisfied and profitable customer base, are more successful at innovating and have a more committed and satisfied workforce.

Because these benefits of being market oriented are so appealing, it is important for organisations to understand the conditions under which they are more likely to become market oriented. In other words, what are some of the things a business can do in order to facilitate the development of a market orientation? Again, much research has been carried out to answer this question, and figure 4 outlines some of the main findings.

First, for an organisation to become market oriented, it is important that support for a market orientation comes from the top of the organisational hierarchy. Market orientation is ultimately a culture or philosophy of doing business and is therefore heavily influenced by top management. If the leaders of an organisation do not believe in and do not actively encourage a market orientation, it is a lot more difficult for that business to become truly market oriented. For this reason, firms where top management has some background or experience in marketing are more likely to become market oriented.

Figure 4: What can facilitate the development of a market orientation?

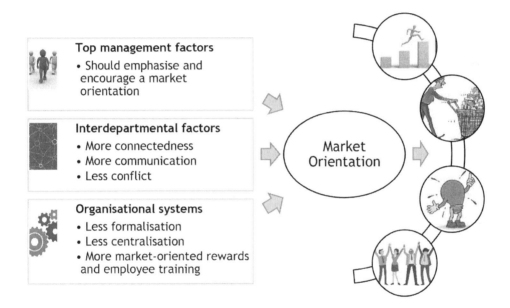

Second, it is also important to design the organisation in such a way that conflict is avoided among the different functions, and communication is encouraged. Different functions and people across the organisation must have as many connections as possible. Thus, both formal and informal ways of facilitating communication among employees are required. This is very important in particular to foster the dissemination of market intelligence. For example, at the Ritz-Carlton, every day starts with a 15-minute employee "line-up", where colleagues share "wow stories" about things they have done to delight customers. These stories regularly feature customer-direct information, such as letters received after a cus-

17

tomer's stay. This acts as a powerful communication, training, and motivational tool, and helps develop an organisational climate where employees learn from each other, and genuinely focus on delivering outstanding customer experiences.

Third, the appropriate organisational systems must also be in place. This can entail reducing formalisation and centralisation of decision making, for example by empowering front-line employees and ensuring that they are trained and rewarded for creating customer value. Again, the Ritz-Carlton provides a good example of an organisation that has understood that employee empowerment is a win-win. The company, which has become synonymous with outstanding service quality, a passion for customer centrism, and exceptional customer satisfaction, owes its success partly to the fact that it entrusts every single employee with $2,000 to spend on a guest at any time to solve a problem without approval from their general manager. By doing so, it has reduced formalisation and centralisation, which, coupled with proper employee training and rewards, and guidelines for service failure recovery, has made it a very market-oriented business. WestJet, the successful Canadian airline, has also minimised formalisation and centralisation, and has given its frontline employees broad freedom to correct service deficiencies.

All these factors have been shown to facilitate the development of market orientation and thus represent a first step for any firm wishing to improve its ability to generate, disseminate and respond to market intelligence effectively and efficiently.

2.4 THE ROLE OF MARKETING WITHIN THE FIRM, AND THE IMPORTANCE OF INTERNAL MARKETING

It should be clear by now that marketing is more than just advertising, packaging decisions and the like. In fact, marketing can play a dual role within businesses. It can be (1) a distinct organisational entity, embodied in the marketing department, or it can also be (2) an orientation, i.e., a culture, or philosophy of doing business, as implemented through a company-wide market orientation. The latter view involves thinking of marketing less as something "to do" and more as a way of "thinking". Many companies have achieved success within their industries by adopting a marketing mindset, rather than thinking of marketing purely as a set of tactical decisions. To be market oriented everyone throughout the organisation has to adopt a marketing mindset and see themselves as part of an integrated process geared towards creating value for customers.

What is often neglected, however, is the fact that this mindset and external focus also requires an internal focus. As a result of focusing on market-based factors, businesses may disregard that market orientation starts from within the organisation. Simply put, a business cannot even start thinking about satisfying its external customers until it has created a satisfied internal customer base and has configured the business accordingly. Yet, few organisations wishing to become market orientated start with internal marketing efforts and HR policies that are geared towards the market or implement sufficient change management to support and facilitate a market orientation. Luckily, however, there are a few guidelines that management can observe to use internal marketing and HR policies to facilitate a market orientation, and to configure the organisation to support such orientation.

One of the most important things to realise is that a market orientation, though perhaps mainly implemented at the frontline level, as already noted, starts at the top of the organisational hierarchy. We have seen that without top management support a market orientation can remain an ideal enthusiastically advocated by the marketing team but implemented by few. In a way, top management needs to "market a market orientation", and this requires understanding two very important rules: first, that ideas and change, like products, should not be *sold* – they should be cleverly *marketed*.

Second, just as a company should not take its external customers for granted, it should also realise that internal customers have choices: why should they accept and endorse the idea of a market orientation? It is quite possible that an engineer in an R&D department thinks the company should be technology oriented, rather than market oriented (e.g., by ignoring customer needs and instead offering the market the latest technology every time, under the assumption that that is what customers will buy). Alternatively, a sales rep may choose to adopt a sales orientation in his or her work, and hence fail to think in market-oriented terms (e.g., by lowering prices to generate sales volume, but cheapening the brand in the process). Both the engineer and the sales rep need to buy into the idea that a market orientation pays off in the long term; and that is often not an easy task. To foster a marketing mindset throughout the business (i.e., to market the idea internally to those who will need to implement it), management should begin by understanding their internal audience and their needs, which can foster acceptance from within the organisation.

At last, employees will be curious about how becoming market oriented generates value for them. They will want to know how being market oriented will make their life easier, help them meet their other commitments, increase their influence, reduce their stress, or help them produce measurable results, etc. They may also want to know what time and effort it will require, what the risks of failure are, and whether there are any career risks associated with it. In other words, they will ask: "what's in it for me?" Management needs to be able to answer this question from the very start, and if necessary, test market key ideas with a subset of internal customers.

Marketing ideas might also entail leveraging the company's or manager's own internal brand. Just as the sender of any commercial message can use its brand equity to get and hold attention from its target market, management can leverage its own brand equity (and the brand equity of the ideas it plans to implement) internally. An important step in developing market orientation is to ensure that internal customers have the right type of experiences with the advocates of the new mindset, the change process, and the message sources; this can ensure that the desired thoughts, feelings, beliefs and perceptions are induced. To this end, managers need to make sure that employees have strong and favourable views of the key advocates of market orientation. Second, they need to focus on how the new mindset will create some tangible difference for both the organisation and its employees. Third, management needs to make employees familiar with such favourable differences. And fourth, they need to monitor the internal customer's responses to its messages systematically, to ensure that the right associations are built and reinforced within the mind of employees.

The development and implementation of a market orientation also requires managing the company's human resources with a view towards developing the appropriate organisational culture. The HR and marketing functions need to cooperate to facilitate the conditions that are beneficial to a market orientation. First of all, they have to take the lead within the firm in improving interdepartmental dynamics. These may include activities designed to reduce interfunctional conflict, improve connectedness, and engender a genuine interest and concern for the ideas of other departments and people. Second, HR and marketing should strive to design organisational systems that are more market focused. For instance, they could design and enforce a market-based reward system. Salespeople should not be encouraged to close a sale "no matter what"; they should be encouraged to create value for customers by delighting them, so that they will willingly come back and recommend the business to others. Similarly, executives should be rewarded for creating growth not through aggressive promotion and pricing strategies, but through a great customer experience. Put differently, growth should be earned, not bought. A good example of such strategy in action is at General Electric, that connected the bonuses of executives to the Net Promoter Score (NPS). The NPS (discussed in chapter 6) measures the extent to which the company is able to convert customers into "promoters" (loyal enthusiasts who keep buying and urge others to do the same), and minimise the number of "detractors" (unhappy customers trapped in a bad relationship who slow down growth).

In short, high performance marketing involves adopting a market orientation, rather than thinking of marketing purely as a distinct department responsible for tactical decisions. The performance benefits for those companies that actively set out to become market oriented are compelling. However, this external focus may yield problems; for instance, it could force businesses into an obsession with the market. The obsession should be linked to internal focus as well, to make sure it does not become an unhealthy obsession.

A market orientation starts first and foremost within the organisation: it needs appropriate internal marketing efforts and HR policies. First, management needs to realise that while a market orientation requires the enthusiastic support and action of frontline employees, it needs to be sanctioned and encouraged from the top of the organisation. Management should not presuppose the passionate acceptance of the new mindset. Management needs to demonstrate to internal customers how a market orientation creates value for them, before demonstrating how it creates value for the company's external customers. Second, internal marketing efforts will stand greater chance of success if management brands itself and its ideas successfully. Third, HR policies focused on the market are prerequisites of market orientation. These guidelines are summarised in Figure 5.

Figure 5: Building a market-oriented business: internal marketing and HRM guidelines

---

1. Market orientation originates from the top of the organisation. Support from the top management is critical.

---

2. Don't just *sell* the idea of a market orientation. *Market* it wisely internally!

---

3. Determine the roll-out plan carefully. Do you need to test-market your idea? Where? To which group of internal customers?

---

4. Communicate the value of a market orientation to your employees. Reduce internal customers' costs and risk and show the benefits. Remember: that's what marketing does!

---

5. Tap into what the internal customer values most and deliver value on that dimension. Your internal audience may ask "what's in it for me?"

---

6. Develop and leverage your personal brand equity. Your chances of marketing your ideas successfully improve when your internal customers have strong and favourable views of you.

---

7. Decrease conflict, boost connectedness and generate an interest for the ideas and opinions of other business areas and professionals.

---

8. Devise and implement market-based reward systems. Avoid a sales volume mentality and reward your employees for creating returns not at the expense of customers, but with customers' enthusiastic cooperation.

---

9. Integrate your marketing and HR efforts. The two should work closely together.

2.5 MARKET ORIENTATION AND MARKETING DEPARTMENTS

The discussion on marketing's dual role within the firm leads to a natural question: If marketing can exercise influence in at least two ways, as an organisational orientation/culture or as a distinct department, which one is more important and how do the two interact? Do we need both?

Marketing research provides numerous good reasons why both may be needed. First, a marketing department may function as the 'evangelist'

22

of a market orientation and act as the 'keeper of the faith'. It can be the catalyst for the diffusion of a marketing culture throughout the firm. The more the marketing department is able to influence other organisational actors and functions, the more the firm can expect to reap the benefits of market orientation. Second, the contemporary tendency of organisations to prioritise customers has caused even non-marketing subunits to learn more about managing the market, and people throughout organisations have become more marketing minded. This marketing-mindedness may translate into more positive views of everything that is 'marketing', and hence also marketing professionals. With such an interested audience, marketing can guide the business and employees through the process of listening to and serving the market, and consequently generate value for the business and its customers. Third, there may be performance benefits of having a strong marketing department alongside a strong market orientation, such as enhanced efficiency, the development of specialised capabilities, growth, and innovation. In fact, studies have shown evidence of a positive relationship between market orientation and marketing department influence. A strong marketing department can still be important to ensure that the positive performance effects of market orientation processes eventuate.

In short, the evidence suggests that to be profitable, businesses must complement a strong market orientation with a strong marketing department. A recent study confirmed that the best performing organisations are those that have both high market orientation and influential marketing departments. Thus, organisations should continue to empower marketing departments while at the same time strengthening the overall customer-centric culture of the business.

Despite this evidence, in recent years some researchers have suggested that marketing as a function is in decline. Marketing departments are losing influence, head count, resources and budgets. In contrast, marketing as an orientation appears to have become increasingly more important, as companies have embraced the notion that everyone within a company should act in a concerted way to create customer value, and that thus, everyone, in a way, is a marketer. Marketing, it seems, is being diluted within many organisations. Some traditional marketing activities are no longer the responsibility of the marketing department, but everyone within the firm is urged to carry them out regardless of their functional background.

While evidence suggests that concerns of a "crisis of marketing" are exaggerated and that marketing is indeed still healthy within most organisations, this trend should be monitored with caution. While it is perhaps true, as Peter Drucker once pointed out, that marketing is too important to be left to marketing people alone, it is also true that marketing people should not be deprived of the function of marketing. After all, we all know what happens when someone suggests something should be the responsibility of everyone. It may end up being the responsibility of no one.

2.6 MARKETING AND ENTREPRENEURIAL ORIENTATION

What about entrepreneurial businesses? How should they organise their marketing activities? This is a very important question to ask, as marketing may be configured differently within organisations depending on their level of entrepreneurial orientation.

Being entrepreneurially oriented means adopting a predisposition to accept entrepreneurial processes, practices, and decision making characterised by a preference for innovativeness, risk taking, and proactiveness. Thus, there are 3 key elements to an entrepreneurial orientation:

1. *Innovativeness*: The tendency of a firm to engage in, and support, new ideas and creative processes which may result in new products, services, or processes.

2. *Risk taking*: The willingness of management to make large and risky resource commitments and hence face potentially costly failures.

3. *Proactiveness*: Seeking new opportunities and aiming to be leaders rather than followers due to a desire to seize new opportunities and shape the environment.

Entrepreneurially oriented businesses take an approach to innovation that is experimental; they try to maximise the opportunities to uncover the random discoveries that occur when all organisational members play an active role. Consequently, under such conditions a dispersion of marketing knowledge and skills may be desirable. Although marketing departments can still play an important role (e.g., at the tactical level), a high degree of departmental influence may not be required, because entrepreneurial firms are in a better position to maximise the performance benefits of market orientation if they share information about customers and disperse marketing activities across subunits, rather than concentrating the responsibility for marketing activities within a group of specialists.

Figure 6: Marketing and entrepreneurial orientation

Firms with LOW Entrepreneurial Orientation	Firms with HIGH Entrepreneurial Orientation
They benefit from the specialised knowledge and skills that come with high marketing department influence.	They have less of a need for an influential marketing function.
Implications:	Implications:
→ Centralise around the marketing sub-unit to capitalise on the marketing orientation -performance link.	→ Having delegates from all departments participate in market-related decision-making is an advantage.
→ Support initiatives aimed at improving the marketing subunit's ability to deal with uncertainty in the external environment.	→ A flat organisation may be preferred.
	→ The marketing department is probably not the source of those innovative and daring ideas at the heart of entrepreneurship.

Firms that are not entrepreneurially oriented benefit from the specialised knowledge and skills that come with an influential marketing department. These firms may need to rely to a larger extent on a very senior marketing manager and a strong marketing group, which can exercise a high level of influence. In contrast, entrepreneurially oriented firms may have less of a need for an influential marketing function. In these firms it may be desirable to have representatives from all departments involved in market-related decision-making, and a flat organisation may be preferred. Employees and social networks that are able to span boundaries are key sources of innovation. To communicate the culture of market orientation within the business, both formal and informal channels should be utilised. In essence, the dilution of marketing throughout a firm is more desirable when that firm is highly entrepreneurial. These ideas are summarised in Figure 6.

2.7 MARKET ORIENTATION: MARKET-DRIVEN OR MARKET-DRIVING?

This tension between a market orientation and an entrepreneurial orientation warrants further discussion. A body of research has developed parallel to the market orientation literature, arguing that organisational performance can benefit when companies are entrepreneurially oriented. However, some observers have argued that an entrepreneurial orientation is incompatible with a market orientation. The former is often associated with surprising customers by offering something they never asked for, while the latter typically entails being responsive to customers' expressed needs. Highly entrepreneurial companies are more likely to come up with products that customers never even knew they wanted or needed. Surely that cannot be explained by a market orientation, which requires being customer driven, and hence respond to customers' expressed needs?

Indeed, the idea of market orientation has traditionally been associated with being market-driven, which involves learning, understanding and responding to stakeholder perceptions and behaviours within a given market structure. In this context, customer needs and everything around them are given, and the firm needs to identify these needs and satisfy them in order to make a profit. This is primarily the form of market orientation that we have discussed up until now. But does being market-driven explain competitive advantage under all circumstances?

Consider for example the Apple iPod, which of course turned out to be a very successful product. Did customers ask for such a product? Was there a need in the marketplace for the iPod that was expressed by customers and was finally addressed by an organisation after constant requests by its customers? Evidence suggests that this was not the case. Not many consumers were "asking" for the iPod, and many were not particularly excited when it became available. Consider for example some of the reactions posted by consumers on Internet discussion boards to the launch of the original iPod in 2001 (Figure 7).

Figure 7: MacRumors: Forums Thread: Apple's New Thing, October 2001

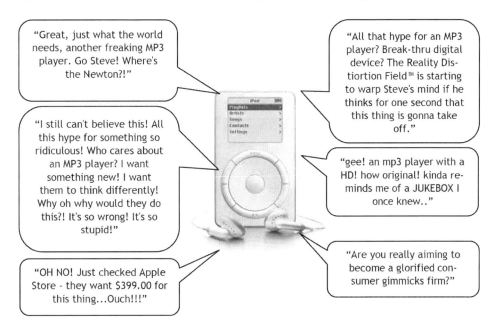

The iPod was not necessarily a very original idea (it was a new product in a crowded market), and most consumers did not see it as something that they had been craving for. The people expressing their views depicted in Figure 7 obviously did not feel they ever needed or wanted such a product. Yet the iPod was revolutionary in many ways, for example because of its simplicity and intuitiveness, but most importantly, because of its integration with the iTunes library and playlist syncing. Apple's hardware and software integration made the user experience much easier and more enjoyable than any other device. Eventually it also made it easier for people to buy music than to steal it.

The iPod ultimately became a notable sub-cultural icon, but the positive elements of the product were not immediately noticeable to the potential customers whose reaction is captured in Figure 7. It was only when customers became aware of these elements (and when a degree of "customer education" had taken place) that many of them felt the iPod was something that they had always wanted without realising it. And that, of course, was one of Apple's strengths: the ability to know what its customers wanted even before their customers knew it themselves.

When thinking about customer needs, we can therefore discriminate between different types of needs:

27

1. *Existing needs*: these are needs that customers have, of which they are well aware, and for which a solution is already available. Opportunities for innovation based on these needs are typically limited and incremental. For example, people's need for personal transportation is addressed by the car, and current ongoing innovation in addressing this need is not radical (i.e., we are more likely to see improvements in the speed, reliability, convenience and comfort of cars than to see entirely novel ways of addressing the need for transportation).

2. *Latent needs*: these are needs that customers have, which they are aware of and they can express, but for which no solution is currently available. Here there are some interesting opportunities for innovation. For example, customers may like laptop batteries that last for weeks rather than hours. They can express this need, but currently no such battery is available, though several companies are already working on it.

3. *Incipient needs*: these are needs that customers have but they don't know they have until a solution to such needs is presented to them. Here there are significant opportunities for radical innovation, but also higher risks. For example, Yakult is a Japanese probiotic milk-like product made by fermenting a mixture of skimmed milk with a special strain of bacteria. Before Yakult could achieve the global success that it did, it had to educate customers that their health could be improved by consuming a small drink once a day, and that bacteria could be good for them. One could argue that customers never really asked for such a product, or even imagined that live bacteria could be good for them (quite the opposite, bacteria were often seen as nasty germs), but they realised they had a need for Yakult once the product was made available to them.

So, one could argue that the iPod and similarly successful break-through innovations tapped into customers' incipient needs. The companies involved were able to identify customers' needs before customers even did. In fact, consumers are sometimes unable to express a need for really new products, or they simply do not know what they want. As Henry Ford once famously said: "if I had asked my customers what they wanted, they would have said a faster horse"; the idea of the car was something that customers could understand only after they had seen one.

For these reasons, we can argue that market orientation can actually take two different forms: market-driven or market-driving.

1. *Market-driven*: this approach to market orientation entails understanding and reacting to the preferences and behaviours of players (e.g., customers) within a given market structure. This approach usually leads to incremental innovation and infrequently produces radical innovation.

2. *Market-driving*: this approach involves influencing the structure of the market and/or the behaviour of market players (e.g., customers, competitors, channel members) in a direction that enhances the competitive position of the business. It can involve eliminating players or changing the mind-set or expectations of customers. Market driving companies (often new entrants into an industry) deliver a leap in customer value through a unique business system. Market-driven approaches entail higher risk (and are therefore often relied upon by highly entrepreneurial businesses), but also offer a firm the potential to create a blue ocean strategy (i.e., open up a new market space and create new demand), revolutionise an industry and reap vast rewards.

A market-driving approach can help business avoid the perils of being overly market-driven. IBM provides a good example of these perils. In the 1980s and 90s IBM was very market-driven and continued to ask its customers what they wanted. Its customers (mainly large blue-chip companies) were interested in large mainframe computers and demanded continuous improvements in these machines. IBM duly gave its customers what they asked for and became heavily focused on large hardware. But by addressing the needs of its served market, and by focusing largely on mainframes, IBM failed to detect and capitalise on several new trends, such as the growth of the PC workstation and software. IBM was late to realise that decision-making and purchase power were shifting away from a few experts within large corporations to the mass market. Thus, its obsession with being market-driven led to several missed opportunities. This phenomenon is often referred to as "the tyranny of the served market": i.e., the tendency for a company to focus too much on an existing set of customers and their expressed needs, at the expense of potential new customers with less prevalent or obvious needs.

Take on the other hand companies such as IKEA, ZARA, Uber and AirBnB. Their success has been based on radical business innovation through market-driving approaches, by changing the way customers think and shop

29

for furniture, buy designer clothes, hire transportation, or book accommodation. One could argue that nobody really asked for these products and services. Yet, once they were made available, customers realised they had a need for them!

Figure 8 summarises the two approaches in a framework that uses two dimensions: market structure and market behaviour.

Figure 8: Market-driven vs Market-driving strategy

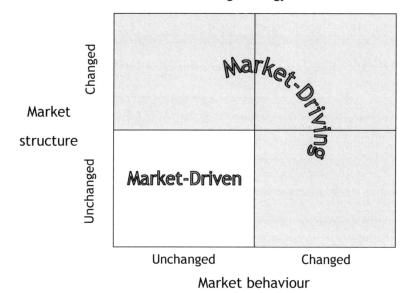

Market structure refers to the set of players in the market (e.g., suppliers, competitors, channel members, etc.) and the roles played by them in the value chain. Market-driven companies usually take the market structure as a given. They do not try to shape the market. Market-driving companies, in contrast, often like to try to change their industry, by changing the roles played by players, getting new players to enter the industry, etc.

Market behaviour refers to the behaviour of players in the industry value chain, particularly the customer, but also intermediaries, retailers, competitors, etc. Again, market-driven companies usually take behaviour as a given (e.g., how, when and why customers purchase a product). In contrast, market-driving firms like to change their customers' perceptions of

30

the firm's offering versus competitors' offerings. This might mean focusing on attributes that were previously not considered by customers or providing new-to-the-world offerings.

When EasyJet, the European low-cost airline, launched in the United Kingdom it was the first airline in the world to cut the middleman out completely by refusing to work with travel agencies. By doing so, it didn't take the market structure as a given (and specifically the channel on which airlines had historically relied to connect with customers) and instead changed it in accordance with its market-driving strategy.

IKEA reinvented what a furniture supplier does and how consumers choose to furnish their homes. To obtain more affordable and utilitarian products, customers give up durability, in-store customer service and product delivery. In doing so, IKEA shaped how the market thinks and behaves. It shaped our view of furniture as something durable into something less durable (almost a consumable that can be replaced more frequently) and possibly less emotional. Also, consider how the store layout forces customers to behave in a pre-determined way during the shopping experience, not to mention how IKEA contributed to millions of people around the world spending their weekends assembling flat-packed furniture. Clearly, IKEA provides an apt example of a market-driving strategy designed to shape market behaviour.

AirBnB, the peer-to-peer service where people advertise private spaces all over the world to be rented short-term, experienced incredible growth due to its market-driving strategy. Not only has it changed how consumers look for and book accommodation, or even what constitutes a good, more personal place to stay when travelling, but it also shook up the entire hotel industry by refusing to play according to the traditional rules of the game. The company is arguably the world's largest accommodation provider, yet it owns no real estate.

So, what is the best strategy for a company? Market-driven or market-driving? It depends on several factors. Clearly, a market-driving strategy can yield incredible returns, because it can tap into an uncontested market space and even create an entirely new market where the company enjoys a first-mover advantage. However, it is of course very risky, as all radical innovation efforts often are. In contrast, a market-driven strategy, though it typically leads to less radical innovation and more modest growth, is safer and less risky. Many organisations have realised that a balanced approach between the two is desirable. They will invest in market-driven activities to capitalise on the current potential of existing products and markets. These often represent their cash cows, which generate capital to be invested into market-driving projects with future potential. In other words, a market-driven approach to market orientation pays the bills; while a market-driving approach to market orientation can make you grow.

2.8 UNCOVERING CUSTOMER NEEDS THROUGH MARKET RESEARCH

In a market-oriented company, strategic decisions are driven by customers' needs and wants, and thus market research plays a central role in generating the market intelligence necessary to achieve this objective. In general, marketers tend to use both quantitative and qualitative research methods. Quantitative research involves means such as structured surveys or questionnaires, while qualitative methods include focus groups, observations, open-ended interviews and field or laboratory experiments. There are significant methodological differences between the two approaches. Quantitative research involves a large number of respondents and explores the degree to which phenomena possess particular properties. This ensures objectivity, generalisability and replicability of the data gathered, and allows for statistical analyses. In general, the main weakness of this approach is that it decontextualises human behaviour and ignores the effect of variables which are not included in the study. Quantitative research therefore lacks depth and detail.

Qualitative studies, on the other hand, yield a wealth of descriptive data and often contain quotations from customer responses. Contrary to quantitative research, that looks at the frequency of phenomena, qualitative research analyses the nature of phenomena. Due to comparatively small sample sizes, data does not lend itself to statistical analysis (and is not designed to do so), but rather helps to gain a better understanding of behaviours. At a time when marketers are increasingly under pressure to uncover the benefits customers seek from products and develop offerings that truly deliver these benefits, research designed to offer rich insights into consumer behaviour is becoming increasingly more important. Nevertheless, a shortcoming of qualitative research lies in its time-consuming nature, making it a more costly research method than quantitative studies.

In recent years there have been doubts as to whether traditional market research approaches are effective in examining customer needs. On the one hand, research methods that divorce human behaviour from its real-world setting, such as focus groups, have been criticised for producing data of poor quality. This is because informants are believed to behave differently when aware of being studied (this is often referred to as the "Hawthorne effect"). On the other hand, the weakness of research carried out in real-world environments, such as observations, is that it lacks direct interaction with customers. It has been argued that this prevents marketers from getting immersed in the culture of their research subjects, which is necessary to truly understand their behaviours. As a consequence, it comes as no surprise that a growing number of companies are adopting a more innovative research method called "ethnography".

Ethnography encompasses fieldwork and participant-observation, both of which are applied by anthropologists in their study of human behaviours. When doing fieldwork, ethnographers spend extended periods of time with their informants, while both observing them and participating in their everyday activities. Anthropologists believe that human behaviour cannot be understood by mere observation only. Ethnographers need to get involved in the lives of their informants in order to explore how people interact with each other on an individual level, what society they are part of and what impact their environment exerts on them. Behaviour is not initiated for the purpose of the study but is observed as it occurs. These observations are then recorded in great detail. There is a fundamental difference between what people say they do and what they actually do. This discrepancy cannot simply be attributed to dishonesty. A lot of behaviour is tacit, and people do not consciously reflect on or talk about it. What is required, then, is both participation in and observation of mundane, day-to-day activities to truly understand human behaviour.

The origins of ethnography in marketing may be traced back to the Xerox Company. In 1982, Xerox launched a new state-of-the-art photocopier, but users quickly complained that it was too complicated to operate. In order to find out more about the difficulties faced by customers, anthropologists at Xerox's Palo Alto Research Centre in California installed video cameras, filming workers as they used the copier. They obtained some of the most insightful data when the camera captured two IT specialists in their attempt to make double-sided photocopies. Unable to do it, they decided to read the instructions, but eventually gave up. This and other data allowed Xerox designers to implement some key changes to the product design, including the introduction of the now ubiquitous big green button, and some more user-friendly and intuitive ways of interacting with the machine. Senior managers at Xerox came to realise the immense significance of a user-centred approach to technology and the need for market research conducted in real-world environments. Following that study, more professional anthropologists were employed by Xerox to study the complexities of contemporary workplaces. This success with ethnography caused many companies to adopt the same method in sectors ranging from pharmaceuticals to services and fast-moving consumer goods (see Figure 9).

Figure 9: Examples of ethnographic market research

Company/Product	Example of Application of Ethnography
Kimberly Clarke	In the early 1990s, Kimberly-Clarke carried out ethnographic market research in customers' homes to test the appeal of pull-up diapers. The study showed that parents and toddlers considered diapers as clothing and attributed both symbolic and functional meaning to them. The use of pull-up diapers was seen as an important step towards "growing-up". Due to the positive feedback given by the participants of the study, Kimberly Clarke rolled out Huggies Pull-Ups in 1991, which became a highly successful brand.
Toyota	Toyota uses a system called "Genchi Genbutsu", which means "go and see for yourself". For example, Chief Engineer Yuji Yokoya drove the second-generation Toyota Sienna 53,000 miles across North America in order to experience the highways his minivan would be driven on. This experience from the point of view of the customer eventually allowed the design team to introduce features that truly met customer needs.
Cheerios	Cheerios conducted ethnographic market research which revealed that customers were not only using the cereal for breakfast. Especially parents of small children saw it primarily as a tidy snack, which could be used everywhere to keep their toddlers occupied.
Motorola	Motorola ethnographers found that Chinese businessmen working in rural areas with no telephone coverage had developed a complex system of using pagers to send coded messages. The discovery led Motorola to develop a two-way pager for the Chinese market.
3M	Ethnographers from 3M observed how customers use and interact with digital photography. They noticed that when customers wanted to share their pictures with someone, the process was difficult, involving either scrolling through

	myriads of unsorted photos on their cameras, or looking for the few photos that had been printed on paper. This information led to the development of Post-it Picture Paper: photographic paper with adhesive allowing people to stick their photos on surfaces for display.
Pfizer	The pharmaceutical company Pfizer used ethnographic market research to identify what prevented consumers to switch from conventional over-the-counter pain relievers to TX Celebrex, a new product offered by Pfizer. This enabled the company to tailor their advertising campaign closer to customers' needs.
Travel Experience	The Context Research Group, a market research consultancy specializing in corporate ethnography, conducted a study on consumer experiences during leisure and business travel. The study helped hotels and car rental companies to better understand the travel experience and to pinpoint market opportunities.
Starbucks	Starbucks leverages the fact that its employees have constant face-to-face contact with customers to collect customer insights from them. It also takes employees on "inspiration" field trips around the world to learn more about their customers and trends.

Competition in several markets (e.g., technology) is becoming increasingly fiercer, as a growing number of companies try to gain a share of these profitable markets. Constant innovation has become crucial in order to keep up with the competition and to deal with rapidly saturating markets and ever shorter product life cycles. Being closer to the customer, understanding what drives them, and designing products that meet the needs of customers are key to the success of a product.

Ethnographic research can be extremely helpful in areas such as (1) product design (e.g., design ethnography to focus product differentiation efforts on features most highly valued by customers), (2) target market selection (e.g., studying how products are adopted to identify early adopters and barriers to critical mass), (3) innovation (e.g., developing profitable innovations based on observed untapped gaps in the market), and (4) unfamiliar or emerging markets (e.g., getting involved in the lives of customers to gain a genuine understanding of their behaviour in an non-artificial setting).

However, ethnographic market research is not without its shortcomings. Compared to conventional forms of market research, ethnography is more time-consuming and expensive. It also produces a whole range of unstructured data, which needs to be interpreted by the researchers. Hence, ethnography is often said to be an interpretative methodology. Statistical analyses of ethnographic data, which allow for generalisations, can typically not be carried out. Also, due to the fact that a certain degree of subjectivity is integral to this method, ethnography can sometimes lack in validity and credibility. As a consequence, some observers have argued that it is an "unscientific" research method. Nevertheless, it should be clear from the preceding discussion and from the many examples of companies that have employed ethnographic research methods successfully, that ethnography offers insights that no other approach is able to provide.

2.9 VALUE BASED MARKETING

The assumption behind the concept of market orientation is that marketing can be similar to a cultural force within organisations. As discussed, it is a mindset or philosophy of doing business that everyone needs to embrace. However, marketing is more than just an organisational culture, it is also a strategic force. Marketing should provide guidance and input into the strategic direction of the firm, and its ultimate objective is to create value.

The concept of value is crucial in marketing. Everything that marketers do should be guided by a desire to create customer value and financial value. The two value objectives go hand in hand, of course, because the firm cannot create financial value for its owners unless it creates customer value. In this section we are going to discuss the dual facets of value, beginning with the idea that shareholder value is the ultimate objective of a business, and then moving onto looking at how marketing can create customer value to generate shareholder value.

2.9.1. Marketing and shareholder value

Marketers have historically tended to rely on traditional accounting and financial measures to assess their impact, such as sales, market share and profitability. The problem with these measures is that they are largely past-oriented, i.e., they reflect past performance but say nothing about the future and can be affected by short-term actions. This means that long-term prospects are not convincingly represented, and the temptation is to focus on short-term profitability. New product development,

36

brand building and other investments may be neglected because they have no immediate impact on profits, and marketing is seen mostly as a cost rather than an investment.

Consequently, marketers have looked for alternative measures of performance that reflect long-term viability and health. These include measures such as customer satisfaction, brand loyalty, product and service quality, brand and firm associations, new product activity, staff capability and performance, etc. But of course, while these measures are better in ensuring that marketing spending is seen less as an expense and more as a long-term investment, they have their own problems too. They are difficult to measure, and, in some cases, they may lead to too high marketing spending.

Clearly, we need a balanced view to understand how marketing spending can create financial value. An appropriate way to measure the impact of marketing is to think of it in terms of its impact on shareholder value. After all, the ultimate objective of a business is to create value for those who entrust management with the capital needed to create returns. These are typically the company's shareholders or its owners. In a non-for-profit organisation it could be donors. According to the value-based view, the creation of customer value is a means to an end: a company aims to satisfy its profitable customers with a view to generating value for its shareholders so that dividends may be paid and/or the business can experience capital growth.

So, how does marketing generate shareholder value? This is not a straight-forward question to answer, mainly because marketing has an indirect effect on financial value. In other words, it creates shareholder value by having an impact on cash flow, and an improved cash flow in turn generates shareholder value. Figure 10 summarises the principle of value-based marketing strategy.

Everything begins with the right business context. Marketing does not operate in a vacuum but is embedded within an organisational context that will have an impact on marketing's ability to generate financial returns. So, organisational value drivers, such as the company's people, its culture, its values and its systems will have to be managed and configured properly, as they will impact marketing's ability to develop and implement strategies that will have a positive effect on the financial value. For example, ensuring that the company is market oriented is an excellent start, as the strategy, systems, values and so forth that are in place will provide fertile ground for marketing activities to flourish. In an appropriate business context, marketing can generate shareholder value, but it does so indirectly, by having an impact on a set of financial value drivers. The financial value drivers point to four dimensions of cash flow that marketing can improve in order to generate shareholder value: the level, timing, duration and riskiness of cash flow. Improving these aspects of the company's cash flow can help generate shareholder value.

Figure 10: Value-based marketing strategy

Therefore, there are at least four things that marketing can do in order to create financial value:

1. Marketing can improve the level of cash flow

Companies are always aiming for larger cash flows, so much so that this is often the main objective of marketing activities. There are two main ways in which marketing can improve the level of cash flow: by generating sales volume or by improving margins.

   a) *Sales growth*: Marketing can find different ways to increase sales. If added sales are profitable and do not require disproportionate investment, cash flow rises. Economies of scale can be beneficial too: as sales increases, unit cost decreases and efficiency improves.

   b) *Operating margin*: The net operating profit margin after tax provides a balance between sales growth and the costs incurred. There are at least three ways in which marketing can improve the operating margin: by achieving higher prices (e.g., by building a strong brand people will pay a premium for), cutting costs (e.g., by fostering word-of-mouth as an alternative to expensive advertising

38

campaigns) and again, by achieving economies of scale (i.e., aiming to generate more returns out of each unit sold).

2. *Marketing can improve the speed of cash flow*

More and more companies are giving emphasis to techniques that accelerate cash flow, rather than merely focusing on the size of the cash flow. After all, an amount of money made today is worth more than the same amount of money made in the future (e.g., because of potential interest earnings, etc.). There are several ways in which cash flow may be accelerated, including:

a) *Speeding up market penetration*: market acceptance needs to be achieved quickly, e.g. through promotional campaigns, strategies designed to obtain trial, leveraging influencers, etc.

b) *Creating network effects*: the product that becomes the standard in the market will be more successful at speeding up cash flows.

c) *Using strategic alliances*: alliances can speed up market penetration, for example by giving access to additional distribution.

d) *Building loyalty*: when customers develop a preference for a brand, they may become more loyal and adopt innovations from that brand more quickly.

3. *Marketing can extend the duration of cash flow*

Some products are just fads, which achieve quick prominence and then disappear quickly. Others are successful for decades and are valued more by investors (e.g., a brand like Coca-Cola). Thus, extending the duration of cash flow can be an important objective for marketers, and may be achieved for example through the following:

a) *Ensuring the sustainability of the firm's competitive advantage*: Marketers need to ask themselves whether a proposed strategy can be replicated quickly by competitors or if competitors can make products at a lower cost. Intangible assets such as brands can be quite powerful in maximising sustainability of cash flow, as they cannot be easily developed or replicated.

b) *Finding new opportunities*: Marketing can help by continuously identifying new market opportunities. For example, can the firm enter new markets in the future? Is there loyalty or preference, which indicate customers will buy other products from the firm? If a brand is strong, for example, a firm may leverage it to enter new markets etc.

4. *Marketing can make cash flow less risky*

Because investors expect higher returns from their investment in risky strategies, marketing can help reduce the cost of capital by generating strategies that reduce the riskiness of cash flow. This may be achieved for example through the following:

a) *Building customer satisfaction*: Building a satisfied customer base can help reduce the vulnerability of the business to attack from competitors.

b) *Generating customer loyalty*: High levels of customer retention may mean that the business does not need to invest much money to look for new customers, and hence cash flow is less volatile.

In summary, when developing a marketing strategy, it is useful to consider its effect on the four financial value drivers. This can ensure that financially desirable strategies are implemented and may also improve marketers' ability to communicate the impact of their activities within the organisation.

Consider for example the success of Dell's strategy in the computer industry in the 1990s. It was based on the direct model (i.e., selling directly to customers instead of through third-party stores), just-in-time systems and build-to-order manufacturing (i.e., Dell ordered parts from nearby vendors and assembled computers only when needed), and superior customer service. The strategy was highly successful because it had a positive impact on the size of the cash flow (e.g., through reduced costs, as parts were bought at the lowest price only when needed, thus improving margins), the speed of cash flow (e.g., cash was collected from customers even before the computer was assembled), the duration of cash flow (e.g., by building a very satisfied and loyal customer base with customised products and great service), and the riskiness of cash flow (e.g., through demand shaping and dynamic pricing, enabled by the direct model).

2.9.2. Marketing and customer value

The discussion above suggests that marketing is uniquely positioned to generate strategies that have an impact on cash flow, which in turn generates shareholder value. The natural question then is: How can marketing improve all these different facets of cash flow? A good starting point is the creation of value for customers. If customers believe that the firm's products or services constitute better value than competing alternatives, they will buy them in large quantities, they will buy them quickly, and they will come back for more. This will impact all financial value drivers. So, what exactly is customer value and how can marketing generate it?

Figure 11: Definition of customer value

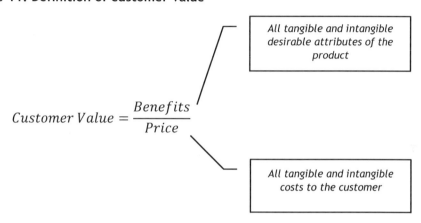

At its simplest level, customer value is a trade-off between all the benefits that the customer expects to obtain from a product or service, and everything he or she will have to give up in order to acquire such benefits. In other words, it's a trade-off between benefits and price (see Figure 11).

This simple equation encapsulates the essence of marketing's key contribution within the firm: the creation of *superior perceived customer value*. Customer value needs to be "superior" because in order to be meaningful, value needs to be higher than that offered by competitors. Also, customer value needs to be "perceived" in the market, because value is meaningless unless it is clearly recognised by the firm's customers. Ultimately, in order to create customer value, marketers need to maximise benefits relative to price to create superior perceived value.

Figure 12: The value delivery sequence

Choose value		
Customer needs	**Provide value**	
Customer value proposition	Product and service development	**Communicate value**
	Pricing	Integrated marketing communications
	Production	Sales force message
	Distributing and servicing	Sales promotion
		Message and media

When assessing the value of a product or service, customers will naturally look at different aspects of value. The tangible components of benefits and price are often straight forward: for example, when buying a car, customers will look at the appearance of the car, its build quality and its price tag. But there are also more intangible elements of the purchase that constitute both benefits and price. For example, a well-known and respected brand name could be seen as a benefit by a driver who wants to display status and sophistication. On the other hand, a waiting list for the latest model of a specific car may be seen as a cost by a customer who would like the car right away instead of waiting months to get delivery of the vehicle.

We can think of marketing's activities in terms of a value delivery sequence (see Figure 12): marketing first chooses a value proposition (e.g., it determines what need a product aims to satisfy and how the product should be positioned in the minds of customers), then provides value (e.g., by helping design the right products and services, at the right price and with all relevant ancillaries) and finally communicates value (e.g., through salespeople, marketing communications, etc).

Often marketers believe that their product is priced fairly and wonder why the product still does not sell. This is often due to a narrow interpretation of "price". Price is not just the money paid for the product, but it is everything that the customer needs to give up in order to acquire the product's benefits. Hence, it can include:

1. *Money*: the entire amount of money spent on searching for the product, purchasing it, maintaining it and then perhaps repairing it if things go wrong.

2. *Time*: all the time spent choosing the product, making a decision, comparing it to alternatives, using it, servicing it if necessary, etc.

3. *Cognitive activity*: all the thinking and brain activity involved in making a choice, doing research, buying the product, learning how to use it, etc.

4. *Behavioural effort*: all the physical effort spent in searching for the product, actually purchasing it, carrying it home, assembling it, etc.

Depending on which statistic you believe, anywhere between 70% to 95% of new products launched every year fail. Many fail because the firm lacks resources, expertise or commitment. But in many cases failure is due to customers' perceptions of the gains and losses involved in the product. Simply put, if the product does not maximise benefits relative to price, it will not succeed.

A key reason for the failure of many innovations is that consumers often reject new products that offer significant improvements over existing products. These failures often stem from a consumer bias: the tendency to irrationally overvalue the benefits of an entrenched alternative and undervalue the benefits of a new alternative. In other words, consumers will look more at the existing benefits that they have to give up, rather than those to be gained from a new purchase. The economists' assumption that customers consider the net benefits of the innovation being offered neglects these significant psychological switching costs. In fact, consumers psychologically overweight things that they currently have and are asked to give up by a factor of 2 to 3 relative to things they do not have but could receive.

This helps explain the success of some innovations and the failure of others. Consider for example online grocery shopping. The benefits are compelling: you can shop at any time of the day or night, you can do it from the comfort of your couch, you can have it delivered, you can save shopping lists and re-order them at the click of a button, etc. However, it is far from replacing the traditional way we shop for groceries at supermarkets, mainly because online grocery shopping is asking customers to give up the ability to select the freshest produce, look at and compare alternatives, buy on impulse, etc. These are all thing we got used to, and we are not necessarily prepared to give them up yet to acquire the benefits of online grocery shopping.

Similarly, electric cars present several compelling benefits to potential buyers. Yet they are still far from replacing traditional cars, mainly because they require customers to give up ease of quick refuelling, driving range, and so on. So, it is not really the financial element of price that is keeping customers away from electric cars (most consumers still do not know what the price tag of an electric vehicle is), it is other intangible elements of price, and specifically, everything customers need to give up from a behavioural and cognitive point of view.

In contrast, consider the Google search engine: it was very successful because it required no major cost to the customer. It worked in exactly the same way as the search engines it ended up replacing (thus, customers really did not have to give up anything when they moved to Google), but provided the benefit of more useful hits, better search results, etc.

There are three issues that complicate how customers evaluate the trade-off between benefits and price. First, the *timing*: while losses are typically immediate, benefits may take a while to materialise (e.g., because of learning, etc). Second, the *certainty*: losses are usually certain, but benefits may only be promises (e.g., long-life light bulbs *vs* traditional bulbs: they cost a lot more money immediately, but they promise long life in the future). Third, an *inability to quantify*: often innovations offer qualitative benefits (e.g., reliability, quality, convenience) for quantitative costs (more money); while the gains are hard to measure, the costs are not.

In short, managers need to ask themselves how much change they are asking of their customers. Product change often necessitates behavioural and cognitive change, and with those changes comes resistance. Sometimes the biggest barrier to product adoption and success is lack of perceived value due to customer inertia.

2.9.3. The myth of excellence

An important implication of the customer value equation is that marketers clearly need to make choices: they need to decide carefully what to offer their customers, and what to ask of them. They also need to be clear about what to give them and what to deny them. The problem is that many marketers, in an attempt to maximise, often blindly, the benefits offered to customers, seek out all possible sources of competitive advantage. This may lead them to try and design the best product, with

44

the best service, at the lowest price, etc. In other words, companies are often tempted to give customers everything they can, in order to appear more competitive. Yet evidence suggests that customers have fairly focused expectations: they do not expect a product or service offering to be the best along all possible dimensions. They want something that does the job reliably and at a fair price point that reflects value.

According to research, successful businesses are those that find out exactly what their customers value the most and excel on those dimensions, while at the same time achieving acceptable performance on all the other basic dimensions. They do not try to compete based on every factor of competition. This allows them to avoid two problems: (1) "me-too" competition, or the tendency for all competitors in an industry to offer customers similar offerings, and (2) waste of resources, because they are not over-investing on product features and benefits that customers do not require.

Businesses need to avoid falling into the trap of the "myth of excellence", or the false belief that a company should try to be good at everything it does. This is the quickest way to commoditise an industry by removing any possible source of differentiation. Consider for example the airline industry: one of the reasons why it is so difficult to be profitable in that business is because most airlines have historically tried to compete on all possible bases of competition (e.g., quality of food and entertainment on board, seat design, lounge access, loyalty programme, network size, service quality, etc). This has led customers to believe that most airlines are pretty much all the same. It is not surprising that some of the most successful airlines today are those, like Ryanair for example, that compete obsessively only on one factor of competition, price, without being concerned with much else.

So, businesses should try and focus on "consumer relevancy": the ability to see the business through customers' eyes and conduct business on terms that customers find meaningful.

As an example, assume that there are five key factors that consumers consider when making purchase choices:

1. *Price*: Customers value honest price. Price does not necessarily always has to be low to be right. It has to be in line with customer expectations and preferences.

2. *Product*: Customers look for consistently good products. They do not necessarily look for the product with the highest number of features, but rather the one that creates value for them

3. *Service*: Customers values services that meet their basic, everyday requests.

4. *Experience*: Customers want to be respected and be offered customised solutions. They will also look at the totality of the experience with the company, not just the individual products and service elements.

5. *Access*: Customers want to get what they want, how they want it, in the right place and at the right time.

Now assume that you are a company wishing to win customers over the competition. It might be attractive to focus on all five dimensions of competition and try to lead the market on all factors (e.g., have the best product, at the best price, with the best service, experience and access). As noted earlier, this is not only a wasteful strategy, but it is also one that is likely to lead to all competitors looking exactly the same, giving customers no clear criterion to choose one company over the other. Instead, organisations need to think in terms of customer relevancy, which means delivering unequalled value to customers on one key dimension that truly matters to them and focusing to a lesser extent on the others.

Research has shown that market leaders tend to share a similar profile in terms of how they compete based on these five dimensions of product, price, service, experience and access. On a hypothetical scale of 1 to 5 (where 1 means the company completely disregards that dimension in terms of investment and resource allocation, and 5 means that the company invests heavily on competing on that dimension), the most sustainable market strategy profiles tends to look as follows:

▪ Dominate on one dimension (a hypothetical score of 5/5)

▪ Differentiate on a second dimension (4/5)

▪ Achieve industry-par levels on the remaining dimensions (3/5)

There are four rules of customer relevancy:

1. The first rule is that an ideal profile tends to entail a score of 5 on one dimension, 4 on a second dimension, and 3 on the remaining three dimensions. A score of 4 out of 5 implies a level of differentiation where the company hopes to use an attribute to persuade

customers to prefer its products, without leading the market on that dimension. A score of 5 out of 5 implies a level of market dominance where the consumer refuses to buy anywhere else based on that dimension. That is, the company delivers the best value on that single dimension.

2. The second rule is that a score less than 3 on any of the five dimensions is not sustainable, leading customers to defect in the long term as their basic expectations are not met. A score of 3 implies that the company's allocation of resources and operational efforts are aimed at achieving a level of acceptance on that dimension. That is, it is assumed that a 3 refers to minimum customer expectations, and a company's offering should never drop below that.

3. The third rule states that domination or differentiation on more than one attribute (i.e., more than one 5 and 4) is not sustainable, resulting in resources being wasted. Research has shown that customers tend to have simpler expectations than we often think, and they rarely look for products and services that excel on all dimensions. Importantly, offering such products and services is often not economically feasible (e.g., low price and high product complexity are often seen as trade-offs).

4. Finally, the fourth rule of customer relevancy states that the definition of a 3 can continually change. Remember that a score of 3 out of 5 means that customers' basic expectations on that dimensions are met, without being exceeded (e.g., the product does the job it is meant to do, but without any extra frills or added benefits). Should any of the five dimensions drop below a 3 out of 5, and hence expectations are not met, customers will disregard any sources of differentiation and will buy an alternative product. In other words, any investment in achieving a score of 4 or 5 on the other dimensions is wasted. This rule highlights the fact that failure to keep up with changing requirements can cause a score to drop below three and can lead customers to defect. Clearly, the threshold value of 3 is not the same for everyone. In mature markets the bar is higher, while in emerging industries or among companies with innovative business models it is lower (e.g., dot coms started off offering very basic services relative to bricks and mortar organisations, but now even dot coms face increasing expectations).

This explains why some airlines have been successful despite competing in a highly commoditised industry. Singapore Airlines, for example, arguably scores a 5/5 on service and a 4/5 on experience. Its access, product and price are arguably all 3/5. In contrast, Ryanair has historically competed with a 5/5 on price, a 4/5 on access, and all other dimensions are a 3/5. Clearly, pairing certain primary (5/5) and secondary (4/5) factors can give a company a competitive advantage.

Part I: Sources, References and Further Readings

Aaker, D.A. & Moorman, C. (2017) "Strategic Market Management", 11th edition, Hoboken, NJ: Wiley.

Auh, S. & Merlo, O. "The power of marketing within the firm: Its contribution to business performance and the effect of power asymmetry", Industrial Marketing Management, 41(5): pp.861-873.

Chadwick-Jones, J.K. (1976) "Social exchange theory: its structure and influence in social psychology", European monographs in social psychology, 8: pp.1-431.

Crawford, F. & Mathews, R. (2003) "The Myth of Excellence. Why Great Companies Never Try to Be the Best at Everything", New York: Three Rivers Press.

Doyle, P. (2000) "Value-Based Marketing. Marketing Strategies for Corporate Growth and Shareholder Value" Essex: John Wiley & Sons Ltd.

Elliott, J.E. (2000) "Adam Smith's Conceptualization of Power, Markets, and Politics", Review of Social Economy, 58(4): pp.429-454.

Hunt, S.D. (1992) "Marketing is …" Journal of the Academy of Marketing Science, 20(4): pp.301-11.

Jain, S.C. (1983) "The Evolution of Strategic Marketing", Journal of Business Research, 11(4): pp.409-425.

Jaworski, B.J. & Kohli, A.K. (1993) "Market orientation: antecedents and consequences", Journal of Marketing, 57(3): pp.53-70.

Jones, D.C.B. & Monieson, D.D. (1990) "Early development of the philosophy of marketing thought", Journal of Marketing, 54(1): pp.102-113.

Kim, W. Chan & Renee Mauborgne (2004) "Blue Ocean Strategy", Boston, Mass: Harvard Business Review Press.

Kohli, A.K. & Jaworski, B.J. (1990) "Market orientation: the construct, research propositions, and managerial implications", Journal of Marketing, 54(2): pp.1-18.

Lukas, B.A., Whitwell, G.J. & Doyle, P. (2005) "How can a shareholder value approach improve marketing's strategic influence?", Journal of Business Research, 58: pp.414-422.

MacRumors, (2001) "Apple's New Things" https://forums.macrumors.com/threads/apples-new-thing-ipod.500/

Merlo, O. (2011) "The influence of marketing from a power perspective", European Journal of Marketing, 45(7/8): pp.1152-1171.

Merlo, O. & Auh, S. (2010) "Marketing's influence in Australian firms: A review and survey", Australasian Marketing Journal, 18(2): pp.49-56.

Merlo, O. & Auh, S. (2009) "The Effects of Entrepreneurial Orientation, Market Orientation and Marketing Subunit Influence of Firm Performance", Marketing Letters, 20: pp.295-311.

Merlo, O., Lukas, B. & Whitwell, G. (2011) "Marketing's Reputation and Influence in the Firm", Journal of Business Research, 65(3): pp.446-452.

Merlo, O., Whitwell, G. & Lukas, B. (2004) "Power and Marketing", Journal of Strategic Marketing, 12(4): pp.207-218.

Ocasio, W. & Joseph, J. (2008) "Rise and Fall- or Transformation? The Evolution of Strategic Planning at the General Electric Company, 1940-2006", Long Range Planning, 41: pp.248-272.

Srivastava, R.K., Shervani, T.A. & Fahey, L. (1997) "Driving shareholder value: the role of marketing in reducing vulnerability and volatility of cash flows", Journal of Market Focused Management, 2(1): pp.49-64.

Woodruff, R.B. (1997) "Customer Value: The next source for competitive advantage", Journal of the Academy of Marketing Science, 25(2): 139-153.

Zeithaml, V.A. (1988) "Consumer Perceptions of Price, Quality, and Value: A Means-End Model and Synthesis of Evidence", Journal of Marketing, 52 (July): 2-22.

Part II: Implementing the Marketing Strategy

3 THE MARKETING PLANNING PROCESS

Although there are many different frameworks and models that set out the steps required to develop a marketing plan, a marketing plan typically involves something along the lines of four steps: (1) Strategic analysis, (2) Selection of strategic objectives and focus, (3) Segmentation and positioning, and (4) Marketing mix. The process is depicted in Figure 13.

Figure 13: The marketing planning process

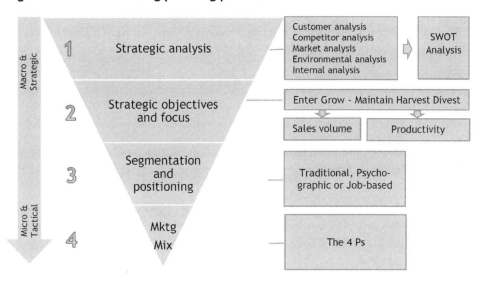

The planning process begins with an analysis of the external and internal environments, which typically leads to a SWOT analysis. Then the business selects a strategic objective and focus, which provides direction for the business's marketing activities. Next, the market is segmented, and once a target market is identified for targeting, the business selects a positioning strategy for its products or services within that market. This is followed by the tactical elements of the marketing mix. Therefore, the

51

process starts at the macro and strategic level, through analysis and identification of broad objectives, and each step of the way the process moves closer to the micro and tactical details of how to make things actually happen.

3.1 STRATEGIC ANALYSIS

An effective planning process is based on a thorough analysis and understanding of information pertaining to the external and internal environments of an organisation. Therefore, the process typically starts with strategic analysis, which includes both external and internal analysis.

External analysis involves looking at outside areas of the business that have an effect on the way the business is run and operates. Areas that need to be considered when doing an external analysis include a customer analysis (e.g., what are the customer segments, motivations and unmet needs?), a competitor analysis (e.g., identifying who they are, how they perform, their image, objectives, strategies, culture, strengths, weaknesses and cost), market analysis (e.g., market size, projected growth, profitability, entry barriers, etc.) and environmental analysis (e.g., technological, governmental, economic, cultural and demographic factors and trends). All together these four elements of external analysis help ascertain areas of opportunity, threats, trends and strategic uncertainties that allow decision makers to put an educated foot forward when planning.

An *internal analysis* in strategic market management has two primary parts. These parts include performance analysis and determinants of strategic options. Performance analysis should evaluate issues such as profitability, sales, customer satisfaction, product quality, brand associations, relative cost, new products, employee capability and performance, and product portfolio analysis. Determinants of strategic options, the second part of internal analysis, evaluate past and current strategies, strategic problems, organisational capabilities and constraints, financial resources and constraints, strengths and weakness. These can be measured by asking the question: how is the company doing in building loyalty from customer satisfaction? Are the products and services delivering value to customers as intended? Is there a cost advantage/disadvantage in production, design or wages? Do we have the type, and enough of the right type, of people to support our goals?

3.1.1. Customer analysis

Customer analysis is the natural first step of strategic analysis, because it defines the industry and because, as discussed in Part I, customer needs are at the centre of everything the firm does. An analysis of customer behaviour should start with an understanding of customer needs and how customers make decisions.

So, how do customers make purchase decisions? Economists tend to assume that consumers are rational economic persons who know all the facts and compare choices logically in terms of cost and value in order to obtain the greatest satisfaction from the time and money they spend. The assumption is that consumer behaviour is guided by economic needs. But marketers believe that reality is not as simple as economic models often suggest. Understanding customer behaviour requires taking a broader view. Figure 14 depicts the customer behaviour decision-making model.

The customer decision-making process

The customer decision making process begins with (1) need recognition, which happens when customers perceive a discrepancy between their current state of affairs and a desired state of affairs. Marketers need to be clear about the needs their customers have. This involves finding customers' main pain points, i.e., the problems a customer has that triggered a need that we can help solve.

After they realise they have a need, customers will move to the next stage: (2) purchase search, where they process available information to find out what they feel is the best solution to their need. Here the customer may rely on any sources of information, such as print, visual, online media, influencers or word of mouth to obtain information. Here the implication for marketers is to ensure that customers are provided with the right information, at the right time and in the right place.

Once the information has been acquired and analysed, customers enter the next stage, (3) the evaluation of alternatives, where the products, services or brands available are assessed based on a set of attributes valued by the customer. Marketers need to ensure that customers perceive their products to have superior customer value.

This whole customer decision-making process is affected by two types of influences: external influences and the psychological field, which will be discussed later.

Once customers have made a decision and have identified a product to be bought, they enter the post-decision behaviour phase. Ideally this is (4) a purchase, when the customer forms an intention to buy the brand that creates the most value for him or her. If it's a first-time purchase it might just be a trial. If the product or brand has been purchased before, it is a repeat purchase. Finally, (5) post-purchase evaluation is when the customer assesses whether he or she is satisfied or dissatisfied with a purchase. The outcome is compared to expectations. If it meets or exceeds the customer's initial expectations, the customer is satisfied.

Figure 14: Customer behaviour model

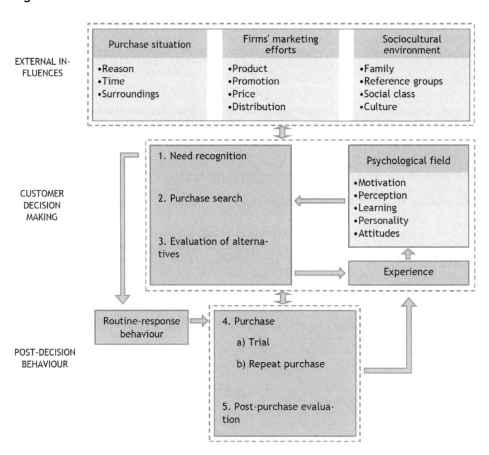

Two things are worth noting at this point. First, sometimes customers do not go through this process as carefully and analytically as assumed in the discussion above. In some cases, customers bypass the purchase search and evaluation of alternatives stages and go straight from need recognition to purchase. This could happen for several reasons, including habit, loyalty, apathy, etc. Brands do like to build a routine-response behaviour in their customers, because it means that no comparisons with other brands are being made. For example, a customer who is very loyal to Apple will only consider the latest Apple mobile phone when they are up for an upgrade and ignore all competing alternatives. This is an example of a routinised response as consequence of brand loyalty, which of course provides Apple with a competitive advantage.

Second, the more customers engage with a brand through their purchase decision making and post-decision behaviours, the more they build up experience with that brand. Such experience can influence the psychological field, for example by improving customers' attitudes towards the brand, which in turn will facilitate the customer decision making process. The more experience a customer has with a brand, the quicker the process next time, and the higher the likelihood of a routine response behaviour.

Customer involvement and risk

Ultimately, whether a customer will go through a long and elaborate decision-making process or a routine response depends on their level of involvement. Involvement varies from customer to customer as well as from product to product. In broad terms, involvement reflects the frequency of a purchase and the degree of risk associated with the purchase. First, the more frequently a particular product is bought, the lower the involvement, and thus customers will spend less time and effort making choices and will require less information. Second, several dimensions of risk can contribute to making certain purchases particularly involving:

- *Functional risk*: will the product live up to my expectations of performance?

- *Financial risk*: what proportion of my budget does this product require?

- *Social risk*: what will others think of me if I purchase the product?

- *Physical risk*: does this product pose a risk to my physical safety?

- *Time risk*: if the product does not perform, will I have to go through this search process again? How much time will I have to devote to acquiring, setting up and maintaining the product? How quickly will the product become obsolete?

The higher the risk, the higher the level of customer involvement. It is important for marketers to know their customers' degree of purchase involvement, as this will determine the strategy and tactics to be used. For example, the marketing communications strategy for a high-involvement service like a holiday abroad will differ significantly from that of a ticket to the local cinema.

The following model depicts the different levels of problem solving according to characteristics of the purchase situation:

Figure 15: Problem solving and customer involvement

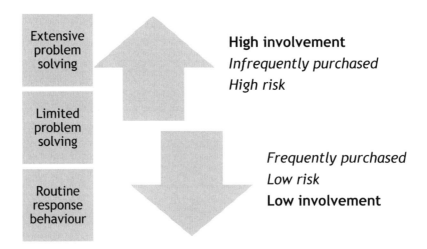

During the purchase decision-making process, customers will engage in problem-solving processes that with varying degrees of complexity, length, etc.:

- *Routine response behaviour*, as discussed, involves regularly selecting a particular way of satisfying a need when it occurs.

- *Limited problem solving* occurs when a customer is willing to devote some effort to deciding on the best way to satisfy a need. It is typical when a customer has some previous experience in solving a particular problem but is not certain which choice is best at the current time.

- *Extensive problem solving* is common when a need is completely new or particularly important or risky to a customer, and much effort is taken to decide how to satisfy the need.

Depending on the problem-solving mechanism employed by customers, fundamentally the job of marketers is to ensure that the process is simplified and that customers are given the right amount of help and information at the right time. In many ways, marketing is about facilitating customers' decision-making process. A key task of marketing is to understand how much help, and what kind of help, customers need to make their choice, and make sure that it is provided to them.

External influences

Earlier we mentioned that the customer decision-making process is affected by two types of influences: external and psychological influences. These influences bear on the customer decision making process by impacting how decisions are made and what the ultimate outcome is.

External influences include the purchase situation, firms' marketing mix and the sociocultural environment. First, the purchase situation refers to why, when and where a product is being purchased, which will influence how customers make decisions. Consider for example the differences in the decision-making process of a customer buying a screwdriver on a weekend from a hardware store to add to their DIY toolkit, versus someone buying the same tool at 3 am on a rainy night from a service station because their car has broken down. Clearly, they will make decisions in very different ways (e.g., more slowly in the first case, and very quickly in the latter). Because the purchase situation can have a significant impact on purchase decisions, it is very important for marketers to keep this in mind when devising marketing strategies.

A second external influence on the customer decision-making process is firms' marketing efforts; that is, the strategies adopted by brands and their marketing mixes (i.e., their product strategy, their communications efforts, their pricing policies and their channel choices). For example, advertising can influence how people shop. So can the particular distribution strategies impact how consumers purchase the products (consider for example how Coca-Cola's intensive global distribution strategy has contributed to making it such a popular drink choice around the world).

It should be noted, however, that sometimes companies can over-estimate the effect their marketing strategy can have on customers. Advertising, for example, can be a lot less effective than other influencing factors on customers, such as suggestions from their peers and other influencers.

This leads to a third external influence: the sociocultural environment. Relationships with other people affect the buying process and customers' psychological variables, such as their needs and attitudes. There are 4 main social influences. First, relationships with family members influence many aspects of customer behaviour. For example, although one member of the family may do the shopping, it is important in planning a marketing strategy to know who else may be involved in the purchase. Other family members may have influenced the decision regarding what to buy. Still, others may be the end users of the product. It is not uncommon in a family to have three separate roles of buyer, user and payer (this, incidentally, is not unlike in B2B, where the product user is often not part of the team that made the purchase decision in the first place). Also, it is important to remember that children learn from family influence and are also able to influence parents as consumers.

Second, customers are affected by their reference groups or opinion leaders, i.e., people who serve as a point of comparison for a customer in forming either general or specific attitudes and behaviours. The growth in influencer marketing is due to the power of opinion leadership. An opinion leader is a person who influences others. Factors that determine the degree of influence include (a) information and experience, (b) credibility, attractiveness and power of influencer and (c) visibility of product consumption (i.e., it's not enough for an influencer to speak highly of a brand; they have to be seen using it). Third, customers are affected by social class, which is typically a function of factors such as education, occupation, income, wealth, social skills, etc. Marketers may be interested to know what buyers in various social classes are like. In many marketing situations the social class groups are quite distinct (for example they may shop at different stores and have different saving-spending attitudes). Finally, culture affects customer decisions. Culture is the complete set of beliefs, attitudes and ways of doing things by a reasonably homogeneous set of people. People within a cultural group tend to be similar in outlook and behaviour. Ignoring cultural differences, or assuming that these are unimportant, almost guarantees failure in international markets.

The psychological field

Besides being affected by external factors, which are typically outside their control, customers are also affected by their own psychological factors. There are 5 main psychological influences:

1. *Motivation*: Everyone is motivated by needs (i.e., the basic forces that motivate a person to do something). When a need is not satisfied, it may lead to a drive, i.e. a strong stimulus encouraging a need-reducing action (for example, the need for liquid leads to a thirst drive). The result of the desire to meet one's need is the product purchase. Marketing managers cannot typically create internal drives in consumers: trying to get consumers to act against their will is a waste of time and money. Instead, a good marketer studies what are customers' drives, needs and wants that already exist (even though, as noted in Part 1, customers may not be aware of them) and how these can be better satisfied. Motivation theory suggests that human beings never reach a state of complete satisfaction. When lower-level needs are met, higher-level needs become more prominent. It is also important to note that a particular product can satisfy more than one need simultaneously. There are four levels of needs:

   - Personal needs (e.g., self-esteem, accomplishment, fun, freedom.)

   - Social needs (e.g., love, friendship, acceptance by others)

   - Safety needs (e.g., protection and physical well-being)

   - Physiological needs (e.g., food, drink, rest and sex)

   This model (often referred to as the PSSP needs model) is based on Maslow's needs hierarchy, which states that people are motivated by a hierarchy of needs (basic needs, safety needs, social needs, esteem needs and self-actualisation), and that they tend to satisfy lower-level needs before proceedings to higher level needs.

2. *Perception*: Perception affects the way in which we gather and interpret information from the world around us. Customers are constantly bombarded by large numbers of stimuli: advertisements, products, stores, and so on. In marketing it is often said that in the West a customer is exposed to 3000 commercial messages a day—though nobody really seems to know where that statistic comes

59

from! Regardless of what the actual number is, one cannot disagree with the fact that most consumers nowadays are constantly exposed to a very large number of commercial messages, both online and offline. For that reason, we have developed some coping mechanisms, wo we do not have to process hundreds or thousands of messages the same way. These coping mechanisms are selective processes:

- Selective exposure: consumers' eyes and minds look for and notice only that information which interests them and, therefore, stands out from the environment.

- Selective perception: consumers block out and correct ideas, messages and information that are in conflict with their previously held attitudes and beliefs.

- Selective retention: consumers only remember what they want to remember.

Have you ever seen an ad, and perhaps even enjoyed it, only to forget what it was about just seconds later? That's selective perception at work. In a way, these perception mechanisms act as defensive barriers to protect oneself from the myriad of commercial messages to which consumers are exposed. The challenge for marketers is to penetrate these barriers with messages that get customers' attention, are meaningful and relevant, and can be recalled easily. That's why creativity, and making a brand not just different, but also distinctive, can be very important.

3. *Learning*: Learning is a change in a person's thought processes caused by prior experience. If a product consistently meets the expectations of customers and is purchased in preference to other brands, loyalty may ensue. Unless marketers satisfy their customers' needs, they constantly have to attract new customers to replace the dissatisfied ones who do not return. Also, in some cases, especially for very new products where some customer education is required, marketers may have to ensure they facilitate the learning process of their customers.

4. *Personality*: Customers act in accordance with their personality. For example, some customers are conservative and will only buy tried and tested products. Others are more adventurous and may be prepared to take the risk and buy first generation products. Lifestyle

analysis can therefore be very important to marketers as it focuses on a person's day-to-day pattern of living, as expressed in that person's activities, interests and opinions. It assumes that marketers can plan more effective strategies if they know more about their target markets. It has been particularly effective in providing ideas for targeted communication.

5. *Attitudes*: An attitude is a person's enduring point of view towards something, which may be a product, an advertisement, a company, or an idea. Attitudes affect the selective processes, learning and, eventually, the buying decisions that people make. Attitudes have three levels:

- Cognitive (beliefs and thoughts about something)

- Affective (emotions towards something)

- Behavioural (intentions to act towards something)

Attitudes usually involve liking or disliking something and often have some direct-action implications. Beliefs, on the other hand, are not so action oriented. A belief is a person's opinion about something; it may help shape a consumer's attitudes, bout does not necessarily involve any liking or disliking. Beliefs about a product may have a positive or negative influence in shaping consumers' attitudes.

3.1.2. Competitor analysis

The second step of strategic analysis involves analysing the competitive landscape. Here the focus is on identifying threats, opportunities or strategic uncertainties created by existing or potential competitors. The key steps of the process involve (1) identifying current and potential competitors, and (2) understanding competitors and their strategies.

When identifying their competitors, many businesses are often concerned with the wrong competitors. Thus, the subsequent analysis is not as useful as it could be. For example, there is a tendency to focus on the most direct and obvious competitors, which can lead to missing threats and challenges emerging from less visible competitors. There is increasing need to identify and participate in new competitive forms as they emerge. For example, colas are no longer as dominant in the soft drink industry, and profits decrease as competition increases. It would be a mistake for a company like Coca-Cola and Pepsi to be only concerned with each other. Other profitable niches have developed in the soft drink industry. So, companies would be well advised to look at two factors when identifying competitors:

1. *Customer choices*: Look at competition from the point of view of customers. What choices are customers making? For example, someone who just bought a 6-pack of Pepsi may be asked what other brands he or she would have bought instead. And what if those brands were not available either? What else would the buyer consider? This analysis provides a more in-depth and valuable look at all the products that customers can choose from, and hence a wider range of potential competitors.

2. *Product-use associations:* Customers tend to associate products with specific use contexts and applications. For example, if Pepsi is regarded as appropriate as a drink with one's lunch at home, it would compete with other products similarly perceived. On the other hand, if it was perceived more as a drink to be consumed at a bar, it would compete with another range of products that are associated with that particular use.

Of course, strategic analysis should never be static. When we assess customers, competitors, etc. we should always try to focus on trends and changes that may affect our business. So, it is not enough to focus on existing competitors alone, but we should also assess the threat of potential competition. There might be potential market entrants as a result of the following activities:

1. *Market expansion*: A firm operating in a different geographical market may enter our market (e.g., think of the Japanese car manufacturers that entered the American market in the 1960s and 1970. A lot of this competition came as a complete surprise to the local car manufacturers).

2. *Product expansion*: A firm may start making new products that compete with ours (e.g., the company Rip Curl in Australia started in the business of surf boards and accessories and now also competes with clothes and watches, representing new competition to established players in those markets).

3. *Backward integration*: Customers can also be a potential source of competition. If a manufacturer of soup for example started making their own tin cans, they would represent new strong competition to whoever supplied their cans previously.

4. *Forward integration*: Suppliers may also be a source of competition. For example, Intel has entered the consumer market making end-user products, and thus competing with companies that might have previously seen Intel only as a supplier of components.

5. *The export of assets and competencies*: A small competitor with strategic weaknesses can turn into a major entrant if it is purchased by or if it joins a firm that can reduce these weaknesses. For example, when Ericsson had declining sales in its mobile phone business, it joined Sony, who brought a set of new assets and competencies that at the time were able to put it back in the game, at least for a while.

6. *Retaliatory or defensive strategies*: Businesses that face a potential or actual entry into their market may defend themselves through retaliatory strategies. For example, Microsoft has made strategic moves in part to protect its dominant software position (e.g., the infamous case of the integration of Explorer into Windows).

Once current and potential competitors have been identified, the next step involves analysing them in order to assess the threats, opportunities or strategic uncertainties that they represent. To this end, market analysis involves considering at least 8 elements that affect competitor actions:

1. *Size, growth, profits*: analyse the competitors' level and growth of sales and market share. These are key indicators of vitality of a business strategy. Growth and high market share are often a sign of a strong competitor or strategic group (i.e., a set of competitors with similar characteristics).

2. *Image*: determine the image and brand personality of a competitor, as this may be important to develop positioning alternatives. For example, a weakness along one dimension may represent an opportunity (e.g., low-cost, no-frills airlines may represent an opportunity for competitors to differentiate based on quality of service).

3. *Objectives and commitment*: competitors' objectives and commitment can help predict whether strategic changes are likely and what future strategies will look like. For example, does the competitor want to be a technological leader? Does it want to expand distribution? Also, a look at the kinds of patents they are filing can always be useful to determine what they are focusing on.

4. *Current/past strategy*: past strategies that have succeeded or failed should be noted. Failed strategies may not be pursued again. A pattern of successful strategies (e.g., in product innovation or market moves) may help anticipate future moves.

5. *Culture and organisation*: the background and experience of the CEO may act as an indicator. Is it a finance, marketing or engineering driven company? What's the organisational culture like? Is it cost-oriented? What about a market orientation? Is it a flat or hierarchical organisation?

6. *Cost structure*: an analysis of the value chain may reveal where costs advantages may be nestled. This is particularly important for low-cost competitors.

7. *Exit barriers*: these can be significant indicators of commitment, as exit barriers can be crucial to a firm's ability to withdraw from a business (for example due to specialised assets).

8. *Strengths and weaknesses*: they provide insights into a firm's ability to pursue various strategies. They are also important when selecting and implementing strategies. For example, a firm may want to exploit a competitor's weakness, or avoid a specific strength.

3.1.3. Market analysis

Market analysis is the next step of strategic analysis, and its two key objectives are (1) to assess the market (for example its attractiveness), and (2) to understand its dynamics (for example by uncovering important trends). There are several dimensions that should be considered when carrying out a market analysis, and these include the following:

1. *Market size:* The total sales level in the market is important. However, a firm must also understand any relevant sub-markets. For example, knowledge of the value of the total soft drink market may not be very useful if market dynamics occur at the submarket level, such as premium drinks, energy drinks, etc. Firms should also consider the potential market. For example, a new use, user group or more frequent usage could dramatically change the size and prospects of the market.

2. *Market growth*: it is very important to look not just at the current market size, but also its growth rate. What size would the market be in the future? All else constant, a growing market brings about

increased sales and profit, without having to grow the firm's market share. This also brings about a decrease in price pressure.

3. *Market profitability:* how profitable is the market, and what factors might affect its profitability in the future? What is the balance of power, for example, among customers, suppliers, competitors, etc.?

4. *Cost structure:* A careful understanding of the market's cost structure can provide insight into present and future key success factors. A firm that achieves cost savings in an important value-adding activity in the market can achieve a competitive advantage.

5. *Distribution:* what are alternative distribution channels? What are the trends? What new channels are emerging or are likely to emerge? Consider, for example, the continuous growth of the Internet as a distribution channel. It is also important to understand how power is distributed within the channel: who has the most influence, for example, on prices?

6. *Trends:* Any relevant and strategically important evidence from customer and competitor analysis should be considered. For example, the global wine industry is undergoing significant changes, as premium wines grow in importance in certain areas, as well as as new customers discover wine in regions of the world where wine was previously not common.

7. *Key success factors:* what are the assets and competencies that provide the basis for competing successfully? These could be divided into: (a) strategic necessities, which do not provide an advantage, but their absence will create a weakness; and (b) strategic strengths, which are those at which a firm excels, and which provide a source of advantage. For example, in the airline industry, safety is a strategic necessity, while superior service can be a strength.

A model that is often used to assess the attractiveness of an industry and its dynamics is Michael Porter's five forces model. The model (depicted in Figure 16) argues that five forces determine the competitive intensity and therefore attractiveness of a market.

Figure 16: Porter's five forces

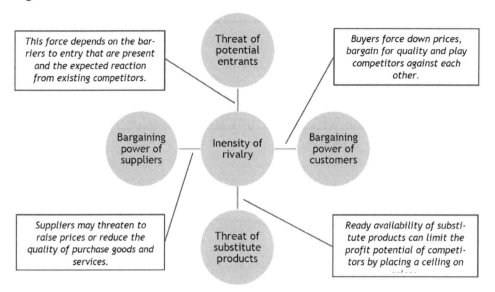

The threat of entry into an industry depends on the barriers to entry that are present, and the expected reaction from existing competitors. Typically, the major barriers to entry might include:

- Economies of scale
- Product differentiation
- Switching costs
- Capital requirements
- Access to distribution channels
- Cost disadvantages (e.g., learning/experience curve effects required)
- Government policy

Buyers also compete with the industry by forcing down prices, bargaining for better quality and playing competitors against each other. This has a negative impact on industry profitability. A buyer group is strong, for example, when:

- It buys in large quantities from the seller
- The products it purchases represent a significant proportion of the buyers purchases

66

- The products it purchases are standard or undifferentiated

- It faces few switching costs

- It earns low profits

- The buyer has full information

A business can advance its strategic position by finding buyers who have the smallest potential impact on its strategic posture in the market.

Suppliers can exercise their bargaining power over market players by pressuring the market with price raises or by decreasing the quality of the goods and services they offer. For example, a supplier group is strong if:

- It is dominated by a few firms

- The industry is not an important customer of the supplier group

- The supplier's product is an important input to the buyer's business

The ready availability of substitute products can limit the profit potential of competitors in an industry by placing a ceiling on the prices they charge.

Lastly, the fifth force, intensity of rivalry among existing competitors, suggests that several conditions contribute to intense rivalry:

- When competitors are numerous, or are roughly equal in size and power

- When the industry growth is slow

- When the industry's product lacks differentiation or switching costs

- When the product is perishable

- When the exit barriers are high

According to Porter's five forces model, firms have several choices to make in order to develop a competitive advantage. At the most fundamental level, companies can, for example:

1. Position themselves so that their capabilities provide the best defence against the existing array of competitive forces.

2. Influence the balance of forces through strategic moves, thereby improving the firm's relative position.

3. Anticipate shifts in the factors underlying the forces and responding to them before rivals do.

A company may offset unfavourable forces by investing in the building of brand awareness in order to raise barriers to entry by creating customer loyalty. They may forge strategic alliances with suppliers and distributors in order to raise barriers to entry. They may invest in relationship marketing, to ward off any threat posed by the availability of substitute products. Alternatively, they may integrate backwards to negate the high bargaining power of suppliers, or forwards, to negate the high bargaining power of buying groups.

Porter's model is therefore useful both as a descriptive tool (i.e., it allows us to take a snapshot of the industry and analyse it in some detail, uncovering, for example, a lot of information that can be plugged into a SWOT analysis) and to some extent also as a strategy-making tool (i.e., we can start considering how to deal with the five forces strategically, by teasing out the implications of our analysis).

3.1.4. Environmental analysis

The final step of strategic analysis involves assessing the external environment to identify factors that might have strategic consequences. Such factors are typically five:

1. *Technology*: Technological trends and events can represent both threats and opportunities.

2. *Government*: The addition or removal of legislative constraints. For example, international political developments or local laws.

3. *Economics*: General economic health indicators (e.g., unemployment, economic growth, inflation). But one must also look beyond the general economy at the economic situation of relevant industries.

4. *Demographics*: Age, income, education, geographic location of customers (for example, the growth of ethnic groups, aging of population, etc.)

5. *Culture*: cultural trends can also have an impact. While globalisation is making cultures more similar in some respects, significant

differences still remain, and the global marketer in particular has to be aware of such differences.

3.1.5. Internal analysis

Effective strategic market management requires not only a careful understanding of the external environment in which the company competes, but also an understanding of the internal strengths, weaknesses and characteristics of the business. Thus, understanding the business in some detail is the key objective of internal analysis.

Internal analysis typically involves three steps: (1) financial performance, (2) Long-term measures of profitability, and (3) determinants of strategic options.

1. *Financial performance:* an internal analysis should include a consideration of financial metrics such as sales, market share and profitability. These should be easily measured and can be highly diagnostic (e.g., they can help determine if current and past strategies have been successful and if change is needed). Sales and market share reflect how customers view the product vis-à-vis competing offerings and when they are healthy, they can lead to a competitive advantage, though economies of scale and experience curve effects. Profitability is also a key indicator of business performance, and it can be assessed, for example, by using a metric like return on assets (ROA), which has the formula: ROA = Profits/Assets. In Part I of this book we also looked at shareholder value as a key indicator of performance. It is also recommended that an analysis of financial performance includes an assessment of the financial value drivers (level, timing, duration and riskiness of cash flow) and shareholder value creation.

2. *Long-term measures of performance:* The problem with traditional financial performance metrics is that they can be too past-oriented and fail to take into consideration long-term prospects. Measures such as sales and market share can be improved quickly in the short-term, often at the expense of future profitability (for example, a company could quickly boost sales and market share by slashing prices, which might work in the short term, but will reduce brand and quality perception in the long term). Thus, it is important to also focus on measures that reflect the long-term performance of the business, such as customer satisfaction, loyalty, product and service quality, brand associations and perceptions, new product

development activity, and employee capabilities and performance. While these factors may be harder to measure than financial performance metrics, they are helpful in managing for the future.

3. *Determinants of strategic options*: A third element of internal analysis should be a consideration of the business characteristics that make some strategic options more feasible than others without major changes. For example, past and current strategies should be reviewed to determine what worked and what did not. Also, the company should review its key capabilities, assets and competencies (which could include its people, its culture and structure) and any financial resources and constraints. The aim of this step is to identify all the relevant strengths and weaknesses which may determine what options are available to the organisation.

3.1.6. SWOT analysis

The output of strategic analysis should lead to the development of a SWOT analysis. In other words, a SWOT analysis may be used to categorise and make sense of the information that has been generated through the strategic analysis. SWOT stands for:

- *Strengths*: the tangible and intangible qualities that enable a company to accomplish its objectives (e.g., strong financial resources, a broad product line, no debt, committed employees, strong leadership, economies of scale, strong brand reputation, etc.)
- *Weaknesses*: the qualities that prevent a firm from accomplishing its objectives (e.g., depreciating machinery, limited R&D efforts, narrow product range, slow decision-making, limited resources, high employee turnover, etc.)
- *Opportunities*: opportunities are conditions presented by the external environment from which the organisation can derive benefit to plan and execute strategies and become more profitable. Opportunities may arise from the market, the competition, environmental trends, and so on (e.g., a strong position within a growing niche, increasing demand for a company's products, availability of a new technology, removal of legislative constraints, opening up of a new market, etc.)
- *Threats*: elements in the external environment that could cause trouble for the business (e.g., entry of a new competitor, introduction of new restrictive laws, changes in customer preferences that may have a negative effect on sales of our products, etc.)

The external analysis should lead to the identification of opportunities and threats. The internal analysis should help identify factors that are either strengths or weaknesses. A good SWOT analysis should not necessarily focus on every single factor emanating from the strategic analysis; it should focus on the most important elements that have an impact on the strategic direction of the business. Figure 17 provides a basic example of a SWOT analysis (in this case a hypothetical SWOT of Starbucks coffee shops).

Figure 17: Hypothetical SWOT analysis of Starbucks

STRENGTHS	WEAKNESSES
• Product and service quality • International reputation • Strong brand • Supply chain efficiency and effectiveness • Excellent store locations • Strong relationships with suppliers • Strong customer loyalty	• Heavily dependent on US operating segment and on international growth • Supply regularly affected by natural disasters and economic factors • Heavily dependent on supplier relationships • Limited healthy options in product range
OPPORTUNITIES	THREATS
• Product and service innovation • New growth platforms • Growth of international segments • Worldwide growth in coffee consumption • Opening of new markets • Decreasing price sensitivity in key markets	• Raising concerns about health impact of sugar and caffeine • Large number of competitors • New market entrants • Growing availability of substitutes • Volatility of price of and supply of coffee • Economic pressures in key markets

SWOT analysis can be very useful to assess the overall strategic position of the business and its environment. Its key purpose is to summarise all the key factors and help identify strategies that will match an organisation's resources and capabilities with the requirements of the environment in which the business operates. It can help a business uncover opportunities that it is well-placed to exploit and manage and eliminate threats that would otherwise catch it unaware.

To elevate the use of SWOT analysis from a mere summary of the situation analysis process to a strategy-making tool, companies can use Match or Convert strategy (see Figure 18).

A strategy could be designed to match strengths and weaknesses, or to convert opportunities and threats into strengths and weaknesses.

A *match* strategy uses competitive advantage to pair strengths with opportunities. For example, in the 1980s UK clothing retailer Marks and Spencer (M&S) had a strong reputation for high quality products, which allowed it to build a strong and loyal customer base that was less price sensitive than some of its competitors' customers. This allowed M&S to gain a dominant position in the high street. M&S decided to leverage these strengths to exploit an opportunity to sell high-quality food and beverage as well, starting with high quality snacks and packaged sandwiches. This approach, and the focus on quality, was a novel formula at the time, which allowed M&S to obtain a first-mover advantage before its model was copied by other competitors. Nowadays, M&S is still a leading player in the UK quality food and beverage market.

A *convert* strategy means converting weaknesses or threats into strengths or opportunities. For example, a furniture maker may be unable to expand its production and distribution because of its small size, high costs and logistical issues. It may also face significant competition from high-volume, low-cost competitors such as IKEA. This weakness could be converted into a strength by stressing their heritage and the artisan nature of their products and making the limited production synonymous with exclusivity. As a consequence, they may achieve high retail prices and strong profits even when losing market share to industrial scale competitors.

Another way to look at this is to consider the following strategic questions (or actions) that match or convert the elements of a SWOT analysis:

- *Strengths-Opportunities actions*: How can we use our strengths to leverage opportunities? Will these opportunities bring about new strengths?
- *Strengths-Threats actions*: How can our strengths counteract or minimise threats? How can these threats be addressed with new strengths?

- *Weaknesses-Opportunities actions*: Can opportunities help reduce or eliminate the weaknesses? Can the opportunities also introduce some weaknesses?
- *Weaknesses-Threats actions*: Can addressing the threats reduce our weaknesses? Can the threats be addressed by strengthening the weaknesses?

Figure 18: SWOT analysis and the match and convert approaches

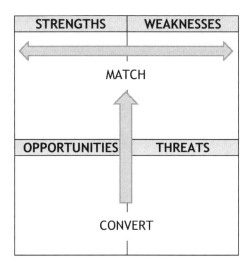

3.2 STRATEGIC OBJECTIVES

The intelligence generated form the strategic and SWOT analyses provides the foundation on which to build the company's marketing strategy. The first step in the strategy development involves determining the key strategic objectives of the business.

In Part I we argued that maximising shareholder value is the broad objective of any business. However, a marketing plan still requires clearer guidelines about how the objective of shareholder value creation may be achieved. Objectives are required that are actionable and can lead to clear implementation steps. For example, some businesses (e.g., new ventures with plenty of future potential) may be seen as very valuable even though profits are not expected for years. The appropriate objective for these businesses is sales growth in the long term. In other businesses (e.g., mature or declining products) shareholder value creation may be achieved by focusing on maximising short-term cash flow while letting the business decline.

Figure 19: The strategic characterisation matrix

DIFFERENTIAL ADVANTAGE

	Disadvantaged	Average	Advantaged
High	Divest/Grow	Grow	Grow/Enter
Medium	Harvest	Maintain	Grow
Low	Divest	Harvest	Maintain

MARKET ATTRACTIVENESS

Therefore, after a thorough strategic analysis, the process of strategic market management typically continues with an assignment of strategic objectives to a business unit. Assigning an objective to a business unit depends on a variety of factors and should always be based on a careful assessment of all internal and external factors that can have an impact on the firm's marketing strategy. A useful model to determine the strategic objectives of a business is the strategic characterisation matrix, depicted in Figure 19.

This framework suggests that two factors, namely the level of market attractiveness and whether the business possesses a differential advantage, determine the choice of strategic objective for the business. The possession of a differential advantage refers to the extent to which a company has an advantage over the competition that creates a significant difference in the marketplace. For example, such advantage may originate from a superior product, superior customer service or a lower price. An appropriate way to assess whether a business has a differential

74

advantage is to assess whether it has a 5-4-3-3-3 profile (as discussed earlier in the customer relevancy model), that provides the customer with something valuable and relevant, while at the same time affording the company an advantage in the market. The level of market attractiveness, on the other hand, is assessed through a careful and systematic strategic analysis.

Depending on the position of the business unit on the two dimensions, specific strategic objectives may be assigned. Business units in attractive markets and with a strong differential position are more likely to generate good returns. In contrast, it is more difficult to make decisions when a business falls in the middle or when one dimension is high while the other is low. The top right corner is clearly a very desirable position.

The five strategic objectives that can be allocated to a business are the following:

- *Divest*: This is about exiting from markets or market segments that no longer offer profit potential. It is about rationalising unprofitable products, cutting costs and reducing complexity. Advantages include the ability to cut costs, a more efficient use of resources, and reduction in complexity and the ability to focus on more profitable parts of the business. This market strategy is ideal under a combination of high market attractiveness and disadvantaged position (for example, IBM faced a similar scenario in the laptop computer market and decided to sell the Thinkpad brand to Lenovo). It is also desirable under conditions of low market attractiveness and disadvantaged position (consider for example a small manufacturer of cigarettes that may decide to invest in a more attractive market). Finally, a divest objective could also be set when another company values the business more highly than the current owner, whether due to better ability to manage the business, or because of over optimistic expectations (consider, for example, the sale of Hotmail to Microsoft in December 1997 for a reported $400 million). However, a divest strategy is not without its risks. Exit barriers may be high, there may be legal issues (e.g., the breach of long-term contracts with suppliers and labour groups), linkages between products may be broken (e.g., divesting from one product means that the other products may have to absorb the costs and assets), and it may reduce the overall power of the company over the distribution channel.

- *Harvest*: This is about maximising the firm's cash flow from its existing assets in a situation where it is likely that the volume of sales will be maintained at present levels or, more likely, declining levels. It will usually be associated with efforts to increase margins and to prune investment. Declining sales volume is accepted if cash flows are increased. This may happen in two ways: by increasing prices and focusing on price inelastic customers, or by cutting down on investment (e.g., fixed assets and reduced stock). For example, Chase & Sanborn Coffee was the first American company to pack coffee in cans. It dominated the US industry for half a century, but the entry of instant coffee and other competitors in the 1950s with aggressive marketing strategies meant that the market was no longer attractive, and the company had no differential position. Therefore, Chase & Sanborn slowly cut down on investment, eventually stopped promoting altogether, distributed its products through selected channels only, and raised its prices slightly. This allowed them to maximise cash flow from loyal customers while accepting a decline in sales volume.

- *Maintain*: This is about undertaking efforts that will lead to current market share being retained. Price competition will be avoided, and an attempt will be made by current players to maintain entry barriers. The preconditions are that the business is making a profit, that the market is dominated by a small number of producers and is not expected to decline, and that there are barriers to entry. Under these conditions, each competitor is keen to maintain the status quo, as changes will always trigger a competitive response. Price competition is avoided, and market signalling might be widely employed (e.g., communication or activity aimed at influencing competitors' actions, such as reducing prices or advertising the introduction of a new brand to prevent a new competitor from entering the market). As an example, the airline industry in many countries displayed this kind of approach by a small number of dominant players for years. However, the successful entry of low-cost carriers often meant that this maintain strategy was no longer sustainable.

- *Grow*: Growth opportunities depend primarily on the firm possessing a differential advantage. But it also depends on the attractiveness of the market. Growth may well be associated with lower cash flows and generally lower profits in the early years, but what matters is the prospect of future returns. Businesses can pursue a growth objective for example by relying on network effects, capitalising on a first-mover advantage, adopting penetration pricing strategies, using aggressive marketing strategies, or simply by investing heavily in building a loyal customer base through the creation of customer value and continuous improvements in their offerings. For example, the online retailer Amazon.com generated losses for nearly a decade after its inception, yet the stock market rewarded it with a strong performance of its shares. This is because investors saw Amazon.com's strategy as an effective way to build a large and loyal customer base while sacrificing short-term profits for value creation in the long run.

- *Enter*: This is about innovation, and it can take several forms. Companies may adopt an enter strategy by developing new products, new processes, new markets, or new marketing strategies. Naturally, barriers to entry will have to be overcome. New products can be new to the company, to the market or both (e.g., an extension such as Vanilla Coke). New processes may entail operational innovations, to save costs or increase quality (e.g., Dell's logistics, inventory and distribution system). New markets might be identified through geographical expansion or segment invasion (e.g., Johnson and Johnson baby shampoo successfully shifted from a focus on the baby segment to a focus on adults). New marketing strategies may involve innovative ways of marketing products (e.g., in the early days of internet service providers, Dixons became the number 1 Internet service provider in the UK by offering a free service and making revenues from taking a portion of the call costs instead—this was a novel approach at the time).

3.3 STRATEGIC FOCUS

Once the strategic objective for a business unit has been determined using the Strategic Characterisation matrix, managers need to implement the marketing direction for achieving the chosen objective. This is referred to as the "focus". There are two types of strategic focus that can be allocated to a business:

1. Increase sales volume
2. Increase productivity

Simply put, shareholder value may be created in two ways: by increasing the volume of sales generated by the business unit, or by improving the productivity of each sale (in other words, getting more value from the same, or even lower, sales volume). Usually, the primary focus depends on the strategic objective, as outlined in Figure 20.

Figure 20: Selecting the strategic focus

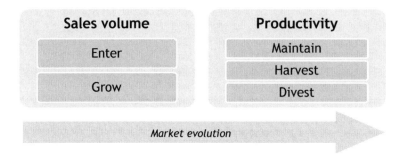

Once a business has selected one of the five types of strategic objectives, it knows what strategic focus it should implement. Enter and grow objectives call for a sales volume focus, while maintain, harvest and divest objectives require a productivity focus.

For example, a new business seeking to grow an attractive market where its strengths can be deployed, should implement a marketing focus geared towards building sales volume. While this does not give that business a licence to be wasteful, the business will tend to implement decisions that prioritise sales volume generation over productivity.

Note that as the market evolves, a business unit's strategic focus is likely to change from volume to productivity. Furthermore, the two focus strategies are not fully mutually exclusive, but rather, they can be achieved concurrently. Yet, depending on strategic objective of the firm, one of the two will tend to be emphasised to a larger extent.

Knowing what kind of strategic focus to implement is important, because it gets the company a step closer to working out what its marketing activities should look like. A volume strategy, for example, is associated with efforts to increase market penetration or expand the market. In contrast, a productivity focus may require firms to consider ways in which margins can be increased. Figure 20 presents a useful framework to decide the marketing tasks that could be implemented to achieve the desired objectives and focus.

3.3.1. Increasing sales volume

In the introductory stage of a product's lifecycle, or when a product in introduced in a mature market with a strong differential advantage, the focus is typically on sales volume. In this case, the main marketing tasks may be the following:

Expanding the market

Sales volume may be increased if the overall size of the market is increased. There are three ways of doing this:

- *Convert non-users*: A company could try and encourage new buyers for the product. For example, after targeting innovators and early adopters, a company might start targeting the mass market, through trial offers, sales promotion, etc.
- *Enter new segments*: When adopter groups are saturated, a business may start focusing on other segments (e.g., a low-cost airline may start by targeting holiday travellers, but once that segment has been fully penetrated, it may also start targeting budget conscious businesses).
- *Increase usage rate*: Instead of trying to attract new customers, a business can increase the rate of usage of the product among current customers (e.g., a manufacturer of toothpaste may increase the size of its packaging and advertise to customers the need to brush their teeth more frequently).

Penetrating the market

- When there is strong competition, there is increasing pressure to steal customers from competitors. Sometimes a company cannot create new customers or increase the frequency of purchases from existing ones. But they can try to take away market share from the competition. For example, in the credit card business it is not unusual for banks to offer free transfers and interest-free periods if you switch your credit card from the competition.

Figure 21: Strategic objectives, focus and tasks

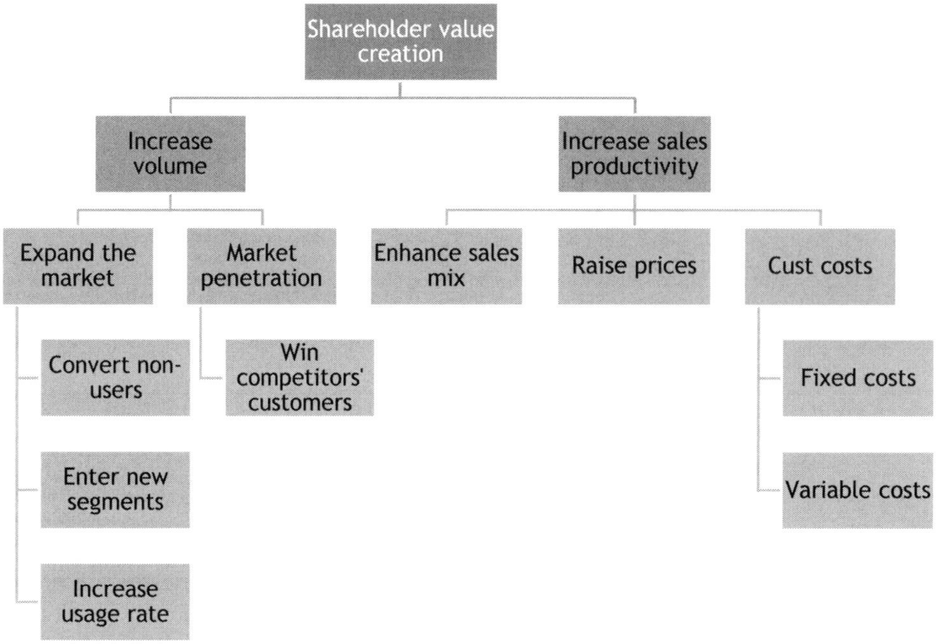

3.3.2. *Improving sales productivity*

As a market matures, competition increases, and customers become more price elastic. Strategies to chase volume become less effective as aggressive moves trigger strong reaction from competitors. It becomes important to increase the cash flow from the volume that the company has already achieved. Therefore, the main tasks are:

Enhancing the product mix

To increase sales productivity a company may choose to offer a wider range of alternatives to its customers that meet specific needs. They may for example segment the market according to the benefits that customers seek from products, and target them differently, for example, according to price elasticity. They may offer customised products that tap into different price levels and preferences. Greater focus can then be given to higher-margin accounts. For example, as it evolved, Dell Computers expanded its segmentation strategy from just business versus personal users, to a larger number of more targeted segments. This allowed them to target different consumer groups more effectively and efficiently. Similarly, a few years ago car maker BMW offered only a limited number of series, such as the 3, 5 and 7 series. Later they enhanced the sales mix by introducing other series such as the 1, 4 and 6.

Increasing prices

Even without improving the product, prices can sometimes be increased. Some price elastic customers will naturally be lost (but remember that this is not necessarily a worry, since volume is not the strategic focus here!), but higher margins may be achieved from the remaining loyal pockets of demand. Increasing prices is common as part of a harvest strategy.

Cutting costs

Of course, cutting costs can always help improve the productivity of sales, especially when it helps improve margins. So, companies may choose to reduce fixed and variable costs. For example, companies in mature markets may decide to rationalise their distribution channel and focus on low cost ways of targeting consumers. Fixed costs are those costs that do not change with activity volumes (e.g., an airline's insurance, taxes, fees, salaries and maintenance costs), while variable costs are closely linked to activity volumes (e.g., an airline's expenses such as fuel, overtime, etc.).

It should become apparent by now that the planning process has shifted from something rather macro-level and strategic (i.e., the selection of a strategic objective to build shareholder value), to something more micro-level and tactical (i.e., the selection of tasks and activities to stimulate demand for our product or to maximise the returns of our sales). The next step of developing a marketing strategy involves identifying target markets and positioning the product or service in these target markets. Once that is done, marketers need to make tactical decisions, which concern the day-to-day management of marketing activities and the implementation of the positioning strategy. This is often referred to as the management of the "marketing mix".

3.4 MARKET SEGMENTATION AND POSITIONING

Having selected a strategic objective and focus, a business also needs to be clear about its target market and the positioning of its products and services within that market.

3.4.1. Market segmentation

Segmentation is the process of identifying and understanding the needs of particular groups of customers. It is a process of market disaggregation, whereby people with similar needs are clustered together into a market segment. Two desirable consequences of this process are reduced competition and more efficient use of resources. In other words, market segmentation is about identifying broad product markets and then breaking them up into smaller groups before selecting target markets and developing suitable market mixes. A market segment may be defined as a homogeneous group of customers who are likely to respond to a marketing strategy in a similar way.

The market can be defined as a number of potential customers who share similar needs and are prone to trade something that is of value to them with the sellers who offer goods or services that satisfy customer's needs. Managers who are market-oriented devise marketing mixes for a specific target audience and market. Getting the company to focus on specific target markets is vital. Target marketing requires a "narrowing down" process, quite the opposite of the production-oriented mass market approach we discussed in Part I.

Market segmentation can be useful for several reasons. First, it can ensure that the marketing mix is more customized to individual customer needs. When marketers can satisfy specific needs, they can ensure that the product is perceived as being different from competing products, even though they may be fairly homogenous. Second, by being closer to a small segment of the market, a marketer can be more aware of their changing needs and hence be able to respond to them more quickly. This may also help pre-empt competitors' moves. Third, segmentation can help save company resources. Often a business cannot serve everyone, so they may want to focus on those customers who are most valuable to them. Fourth, segmentation can reduce competitive intensity by actively avoiding direct competition. It may also help reduce the risk of price wars.

Ideally, market segments should meet the following criteria:

- *Internally homogeneous* – Customers belonging to one market segment should be as similar as possible to each other with respect to their likely responses to marketing mix variables and their segmenting dimensions.

- *Externally heterogeneous* – Customers belonging to different segments should be as different as possible to each other with respect to their likely response to marketing mix variables and their segmenting dimensions.

- *Profitable* - The segment is large enough and can be served at a profit.

- *Operational* - The segmentation approach must be able to be commercialised and the company can reach the customers. The segmenting dimensions should be useful for identifying customers and deciding on marketing mix variables.

At the most basic level, there are three key approaches to segmentation:

- *Concentrated (the single market approach)* – This involves segmenting the market and selecting one of the homogeneous segments as the company's target market. The company can achieve a strong market position, although it may involve a higher risk, and reach economies of scale. For example, an ancient city wishing to foster tourism may decide to exclusively target holiday makers who are interested in historic travel and may for example partner up with historical societies to reach this market and place ads in their newsletters.

- *Differentiated marketing (the multiple market approach)* – It involves segmenting the market and choosing two or more segments, each of which will be treated as a separate target market requiring a different marketing mix. The company can achieve a deep position within each market segment and also strengthen its image in the product category. However, adding products will increase costs (e.g., in promotion, distribution, etc.). Also, one should always be aware that a new product can make an old one obsolete. For example, the city may decide to focus on three segments at the same time: families with children (for instance, by promoting to kids and their parents the importance to learn about history), the elderly (who may be more likely to be members of historical societies and may be reached through newsletters and events) and backpackers (by using influencer marketing or advertising during student events, with an emphasis on elements such as availability of low-cost accommodation, entertainment in a picturesque environment, adventure, etc.).

- *Undifferentiated marketing* - Segmentation is ignored, and the whole market is regarded as the target. Advantages are provided by economies of scale, while a disadvantage is represented by a larger competition. For example, the city targets everyone who may be interested in visiting it with the same message (e.g., building awareness of the city through mainstream TV and newspaper advertising).

Marketers who follow the first two approaches are often called segmenters, while those who use the third are called combiners. When deciding on the best segmentation strategy, the following factors should be considered:

1. Resources: when resources are limited, concentrated marketing is most appropriate.

2. Product homogeneity: products that are very similar are suited to undifferentiated markets.

3. Stage in the product's life cycle: new products are often launched in only one version and are fairly undifferentiated.

4. Competitors' marketing strategies: companies may choose to target specific niches in order to avoid an established mass-market competitor.

5. Segment interrelationships: two or more segments may be related, so in some cases the same marketing mix may be used, which can yield economies of scale.

6. Segment invasion: success in one segment can in some cases provide a platform for entering other segments.

There are many different bases of segmentation that marketers can use. These are depicted in Figure 22.

Markets can be segmented according to product characteristics. For example, a business may segment the market based on product complexity, the number of features, whether the product is to be used in professional applications versus the hobbyist market, etc.

Figure 22: Main bases of segmentation

Product-based	Customer-based	Psychographics
Characteristics of the product: Size, shape, colour, technology, features, product application, service, length of life, brand, season, etc.	**Demographics**: age, gender, religion, ethnic group, culture, education, social class, etc. **Geodemographics**: geographical location, urban, non-urban, etc. **Others**: use occasion, place of use, time of use, loyalty, etc.	**Lifestyle**: attitudes, interests, opinions, perceptions, value analysis lifestyle, personality, etc.

Alternatively, the market may be segmented according to demographic variables, such as gender and age, and geodemographic variables, such as the location of the customer. Other variables may also include where and when the product is being used.

Finally, markets may also be segmented according to psychographic variables, such as the customer's lifestyle, their personality and values, etc. The idea in this case is to group customers based on what motivates them to buy products.

A popular psychographic segmentation tool is the Values and Lifestyles (VALS™) approach developed at SRI International in the 1970s and 80s and based on Maslow's needs hierarchy model. The tool uses a proprietary survey method to classify consumers into one of nine groups. The original tool (which has since gone through several different revisions) featured the following nine segments, based on consumers' lifestyles: (1) survivors (economically disadvantaged consumers focused on the basics and immediate needs), (2) sustainers (cautious consumers who have a difficult time making decisions, yet value social status), (3) belongers (conservative consumers driven by a desire to maintain the status quo, and who like traditional brands over new ones), (4) emulators (youthful consumers who are socially inclined and appreciate value and coolness in products), (5) achievers (typically affluent upper-middle class consumers who are self-confident and like high quality products), (6) I-Am-Mes (typically the youngest group of consumers, they are socially active, adventurous and creative), (7) experiential (a more mature, less extreme version of the I-

Am-Mes, who like pleasurable experiences and to try everything once), (8) societally conscious (a self-confident, independent group of consumers who are not interested in social status, are environmentally conscious and prefer simple living), and (9) integraters (consumers who display several features of the previous groups at the same time, and are thus both decisive and introspective, mature and balance).

Another similar tool is the Cross-Cultural Consumer Characterisation (4 Cs) framework developed by the agency Y&R. The 4Cs framework groups consumers into seven types, depending on their core motivation: (1) Explorers (risk-takers driven by a need for discovery, who like brands that offer unique experiences) (2) Aspirers (status and image-conscious, materialistic consumers driven by others' perceptions of them, (3) Succeeders (confident consumers who like to be in control and seek reward and prestige from brands), (4) Reformers (socially-aware and anti-materialistic consumers driven by personal enlightenment), (5) Mainstream (value-conscious consumers who are primarily concerned about security in their daily life and prefer established brands), (6) Strugglers (consumers with limited resources who live for today and make few plans for tomorrow) (7) Resigned (mainly older consumers with stable values built up over time, whose main drive is survival and whose choices are mainly driven by familiarity and a need for safety and economy).

Psychographic segmentation tools like these can be very useful to marketers, for example to study a market (e.g., to understand customer differences in a market and identify opportunities), to position a product, to commercialise new products (e.g., it can facilitate successful product launches and helps avoid costly mistakes) and to communicate effectively (e.g., it can help fine-tune effective messaging campaigns that trigger the right responses in our audience - it can help "push the right buttons"). Psychographic segmentation is often argued to be more effective than demographic segmentation, because it takes into consideration psychological attributes that truly determine how customers think and behave.

However, there is a further way in which markets may be segmented, which is based on the benefits that the product or service delivers to customers. A simple way to think about this approach is to ask yourself: what job does the product do for my customers? Afterwards, you segment the market based on the different jobs the products do. Let's consider a famous example provided by Harvard Professor Clay Christensen.

Christensen tells a story of an American fast food chain that sold a number of products, ranging from hamburgers to sandwiches and from ice cream to biscuits. One of the products it also sold was milkshakes. This was a particularly attractive product because the company benefitted from high margins. Hence, it decided it wanted to try and increase sales of milkshakes.

The first thing the company did was defining the market segment by product (milkshakes) and then segment it further by demographic and other customer characteristics. In doing so, it used demographic and personality characteristics of frequent milkshake buyers to identify the typical customers. It then invited representative people from this segment (i.e., people who fit the age profile, area of residence, personality traits, etc.), to evaluate how to improve the product. In focus groups, the panellists gave very clear feedback about how to improve the milkshakes, for example by making small changes to the pricing, the consistency of the product, the flavours available, and so on. However, after implementing the changes, sales volume did not change. The company was puzzled. After all, they seemed to have followed textbook marketing!

Therefore, they hired a consulting team to study the problem. The team took a different approach. First, they sat in the fast food restaurants and watched. They chronicled when and how each milkshake was bought. In doing so, they tried to understand the purchase patterns. They quickly discovered that there were two main buyer groups: The first group came in primarily in the morning and purchased milkshakes alone quickly and consumed them in their cars. These people were interviewed on the way out, and the consultants realised that most of these customers bought milkshakes to do a job: to make a long boring commute into town more interesting, and to eat something that would keep them full till lunchtime. They were also asked what else they would buy if milkshakes were not available. Donuts, muffins, cookies and fruit were popular substitutes, but they were consumed too quickly and could make the customers' fingers sticky, which was undesirable when driving to work. The milkshake simply did its job better than any competitor: it took customers typically 20 minutes to consume one (which was also the average length of a commute to work), it was filling, and it could be placed conveniently in cup holders.

In contrast, the second group of customers, which tended to turn up mostly in the afternoon, purchased milkshakes with other food such as burgers and sandwiches. Watching their behaviour quickly revealed that they purchased milkshakes not for themselves but for their children, for consumption in the store. Parents were exhausted from repeatedly saying "no" to kids and used milkshakes as an easy way to placate them while they were having their own meal. However, the consultants noticed that the children were too slow to consume the milkshake and parents would have to wait impatiently for them to finish. Thus, for this second group of customers, the job that the milkshake did was to make their children happy and to placate them.

Thus, in essence, the key customers were buying milkshakes for two very different reasons. When the company arranged the focus group, these two groups were averaged together, and the feedback obtained was not very useful (it led to a one-size-fits-none kind of solution). The product changes were therefore ineffective. In the second scenario, the consultants were instead able to make appropriate product changes. First, for the morning customers the shake was made thicker (so it would last longer), chunks of fruit were added (to make it more interesting and to alleviate boredom), and the machine was moved nearer to the door and prepaid cards were introduced (to make it quicker). For the afternoon customers, the shake ordered at the counter was runnier (so it was consumed more easily and quickly by children) and toys were introduced (to ensure kids have something to do while parents eat their meals).

In short, by understanding the job and improving the product accordingly, the fast food chain was able to gain share against the competition, and not just competing sellers of milkshakes, but also donuts, muffins, fruit and boredom. The key insight is that the job that the product does for customers is often the most effective way to segment markets. Marketers should ask what outcomes, benefits or solutions customers seek out of their products, and then segment the market accordingly. This example of course also highlights the usefulness of ethnographic and observation-based research that we discussed in Part I.

3.4.2. Product positioning

Before marketers can establish and implement a marketing mix for their products and services, they need to determine the positioning of the product in the market. Positioning is concerned with the specific image of a product in the minds of customers relative to competitive products. Marketers attempt to position their products in a particular way in the minds of their target markets (e.g., low price, high quality, most technologically advanced, etc.). Positioning is always relative to the competition. For example, Volvo has notoriously positioned itself on safety vis-à-vis other car makers, while BMW is positioned around the idea of driving pleasure.

Figure 23: Developing a positioning strategy

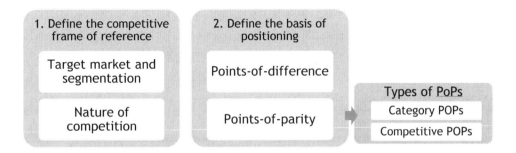

Figure 23 outlines the key steps involved in the development of a positioning strategy. First, the company needs to define the competitive frame of reference. When we segment a market, the decision of targeting a certain set of customers defines the nature of competition. A starting point is to define product category membership and ask ourselves "Which products do we want to compete with?" Segmentation is very important, as customers may be clustered together according to their needs and responses. The company should then position the product accordingly. One should always beware of defining competition too narrowly, as it can lead to missing some competitors. A business entering a new product category may also find it difficult to convince customers that the brand has a place in that category. For example, when Sony entered the PC market, many believed that it was not in the same class as IBM, Dell, HP and other PC manufacturers. Sony had to invest heavily in advertising to reinforce category membership.

Second, the company needs to define the basis of positioning. Devising a successful positioning strategy requires looking at the correct points of difference and points of parity associations. Points-of-difference associations refer to attributes or benefits that consumers strongly associate with a brand, positively evaluate, and believe they could not find to the same extent with a competitive brand. These can come from unique attributes, performance benefits, quality, low cost, imagery associations, etc. Points-of-parity associations, in contrast, are not necessarily unique to the brand but may be shared with other brands. There are two types of points of parity: (1) Category points of parity are necessary but not sufficient conditions for brand choice (e.g., when Nivea launched shampoos and deodorants, it had to focus first on meeting customers' quality

89

expectations in these new categories, and only then, could it concentrate on its unique selling point of "gentle" and "caring"). (2) Competitor's points of difference are negated and addressed through competitive points of parity. They may represent an attempt to break even in those areas where competitors claim superiority as their unique selling point (e.g., the car manufacturer Saab tried to position itself as a very safe car to negate Volvo's advantage on that dimension; in this case, Saab developed a competitive point of parity to destroy Volvo's point of difference).

The two most important considerations in choosing points of difference are that (1) consumers should find the point of difference (PoD) desirable and that (2) customers believe the firm has the capabilities to deliver on it. Desirability and deliverability each have dimensions that need to be managed:

1. Desirability dimensions:

    - *Relevance*: How relevant is the PoD? For example, in the 1990s many companies introduced clear versions of their products (such as colas, dishwashing detergents, soaps, etc.), assuming that clear stands for pure, lightness and natural. These products failed because the "clear" association was not relevant or of any value to customers.

    - *Distinctiveness*: The PoD has to be distinctive and superior. There needs to be an important basis for differentiation (e.g., many companies introducing long-lasting medications found that customers still preferred fast-acting ones, even if it meant taking the product more often).

    - *Believability*: A company should offer a compelling and credible reason for choosing the product. Customers must trust the brand to deliver on the promised PoD (e.g., a perfume positioned as elegant and sophisticated may have to make this positioning believable by endorsing haute couture, fashion shows and elegant events).

2. Deliverability dimensions:

    - *Feasibility*: Can the firm actually create the PoD? A PoD always has to be feasible, or the product is bound to fail.

    - *Communicability*: What verifiable evidence or proof points can marketers communicate as support, so that customers will actually believe in the brand and its desired associations?

- *Sustainability*: Is the PoD defendable, for example from competitive replication, and can it be sustained in the long term?

Finally, the positioning strategy must be reviewed regularly and updated if necessary. Changes in consumer preferences, in competition, or in the external environment might mean that a product's positioning can become obsolete. For example, to take advantage of significant global market opportunities, Korean mobile phone manufacturer HTC repositioned itself successfully from an affordable provider of parts and components used by other manufacturers to an innovative company that delivers "brilliant simplicity" to end users.

In some cases, the positioning strategy might be updated to shift the focus of a product from something functional to something more emotional, especially when a product has established itself strongly as delivering a functional benefit and now also wants to build a more personal connection with customers. For example, for many decades Dove was positioned as a creamy soap that is mild to the skin and contains one-third moisturising cream. This changed more recently when the brand was repositioned around the idea of natural beauty. Suddenly, Dove took a stance in the beauty industry by emphasising self-respect and by urging women to be themselves and be beautiful in a natural way. In this way, Dove aimed to position itself not only on rational dimensions pertaining to product quality and features, but also on emotional aspects that could build a connection with customers at a deeper level.

To communicate a product or service's positioning, marketers often use a tool called positioning or perceptual mapping. The tool highlights distinguishing positions from the competition and should be driven by dimensions valued by customers. For example, consider the car market in a hypothetical country. The competitive landscape may be described according to two key dimensions: first, whether a vehicle offers the benefit of being very sporty, dynamic and aggressive, or whether it is upscale, conservative or classic; second, a car manufacturer may be seen as cheap or affordable, versus exclusive and expensive. These dimensions may be plotted in a positioning map, as in Figure 24.

A positioning map can be very useful to communicate the relative positioning of competing brands in the mind of the customer. It can also be a useful tool to identify gaps in the market. For example, Figure 24 suggests that very few car makers are positioned along a mid-price/very sporty proposition. A marketer interested in positioning a vehicle in that area might want to investigate whether the gap indeed represents a potential for a new brand, or whether it is a gap in the market because there is in fact no demand for such a product. The tool is also useful to help identify a brand's most direct competitors, i.e., those with a very similar positioning.

Figure 24: Positioning map of selected car makers in a hypothetical market

PART II: SOURCES, REFERENCES AND FURTHER READINGS

Anderson, P. (1982) "Marketing, Strategic Planning and the Theory of the Firm", Journal of Marketing, 46(Spring): pp. 15-26.

Biggadike, E.R. (1981) "The contributions of marketing to strategic management", Academy of Management Review, 6(4): pp. 621-632.

Bock, T. & Uncles, M. (2002) "A taxonomy of differences between consumers for market segmentation", International Journal of Research in Marketing, 19: pp. 215-224.

Brooksbank, R. (1994) "The Anatomy of Marketing Positioning Strategy", Marketing Intelligence & Planning, 12(4): pp.10 – 14.

Chin-Feng, L. (2002) "Segmenting customer brand preference: Demographic or psychographic", Journal of Product and Brand Management, 11(4): pp. 249-268.

Christensen, C.M., Hall, T., Dillon, K. & Duncan, D.S. (2016) "Competing against luck: The story of innovation and customer choice", New York: HarperCollins.

Christensen, C.M., Hall, T. Dillon, K & Duncan, D.S. (2016) "Know your customers' job to be done", Harvard Business Review, September.

Hambrick, D. C., MacMillan, I. C., & Day, D. L. (1982) "Strategic Attributes and Performance in the BCG Matrix-A Profit Impact of Market Strategies (PIMS)-Based Analysis of Industrial Product Businesses", Academy of Management Journal, 25(3): pp. 510-531.

Helms, M & Nixon, J. (2010) "Exploring SWOT analysis- where are we now? A review of academic research from the last decade", Journal of Strategy and Management, 3(3): pp. 215-251.

Kahle, L.R., Beatty, S.E. & Homer, P. (1986) "Alternative Measurement Approaches to Consumer Values: The List of Values (LOV) and Values and Life Style (VLAS)", Journal of Consumer Research, 13(3), pp: 405-409.

Keller, K. (2012) "Strategic Brand Management: Global Edition", London: Pearson.

Dickson, P.R. & Ginter, J.L. (1987) "Market segmentation, product differentiation, and marketing strategy", Journal of Marketing, 51(2): pp.1-10.

McKenna, R. (1991) "Marketing is everything", Harvard Business Review, 69(1): pp.65-79.

Mitchell, A (1983) "The Nine American Lifestyles: Who We are and Where We're Going", Macmillan: The University of Michigan.

Neal, C., Quester, P. & Hawkins, D. (1999) "Consumer behaviour: implications for marketing strategy", Sydney: McGraw Hill.

Nobel, C. (2011) "Clay Christensen's Milkshake Marketing" Harvard Business School- Working Knowledge. https://hbswk.hbs.edu/item/clay-christensens-milkshake-marketing

Novak, T.P. MacEvoy, B. (1990) "On Comparing Alternative Segmentation Schemes: The List of Values (LOV) and Values and Life Styles (VALS)", Journal of Consumer Research, 171), pp: 105-109.

Porter, M.E. (2008) "The Five Competitive Forces That Shape Strategy" Harvard Business Review, 86(1): pp: 25-40.

Quester, P.G., McGuiggan, R.L., Perreault, W.D. & McCarthy, E.J. (2004) "Marketing: Creating and Delivering Value", 4th ed., Sydney: McGraw Hill.

Y&R Europe (2010) "There are Seven Kinds of People in the World" London: Y&R Europe.

Wind, Y & Robertson, T. (1983) "Marketing Strategy: New Directions for Theory and Research", Journal of Marketing, 47(Spring): pp. 12-25.

Whitwell, G., Lukas, B. & Doyle, P. (2003) "Marketing Management: A Strategic Value-Based Approach", Milton, Australia: John Wiley & Sons.

Part III: Executing the Strategy Through Marketing Tactics

4 THE MARKETING MIX

Once the strategic objectives have been set, the focus has been selected and the target market and positioning strategies have been decided for the business unit, the next question is: how exactly do we achieve our strategic goals? There are many possible ways to satisfy the needs of the target customers. The marketing mix is a planned mix of the controllable elements of a product or service's marketing plan, and it is commonly referred to as the 4Ps: product, price, place, and promotion. The fundamental idea is that these four elements are adjusted until the right combination is found that serves the needs of the customers, while generating optimum income.

The term marketing mix was coined in a paper by Neil Borden called "The Concept of the Marketing Mix." He started using the term after he learned about it from an associate, who already in 1948 described the role of the marketing manager as a "mixer of ingredients"; a person who occasionally adheres to recipes of others, other times creates his own recipe, sometimes adjusts a recipe based on the available ingredients, and at other times creates new recipes not tried before.

To use a metaphor, imagine making a cake using four key ingredients: flour, sugar, eggs and water. To make the cake sweeter, we can add more sugar, to make it firmer, we can add more flour, to make it runnier, we can add more water, to add flavour, we can use more eggs, etc. Similarly, a marketer can mix the four key ingredients of the marketing mix to tweak the end result of the marketing efforts. Raise the price and the product is perceived as more exclusive, use intensive distribution and the product will be perceived as accessible and ubiquitous, add some promotion to build positive perceptions, design attractive packaging to communicate quality, etc. There are infinite ways in which the four ingredients of the marketing mix may be mixed, and success will largely depend on what customers want and what marketers can do, often in creative and novel ways.

In short, the variables in the marketing mix entail several decisions that need to be made:

1. *Product*: product design, managing features, branding, warranties, customer service, etc.

2. *Place* (or Distribution): channel objectives, selection of channels, design/implementation of channel controls, recruitment of channel members, etc.

3. *Promotion*: communication objectives and methodology, selection of media, budget determination, timing, etc.

4. *Price*: determination of pricing objectives, pricing policy, role of bonuses and discounts, etc.

This is the set of variables that the firm blends to produce the response it wants in the target market. A marketing strategy identifies a target market and establishes a marketing mix for that market. Working out the marketing mix is essentially working out the tactics of the product's positioning strategy.

It is important that a thorough internal and external analysis is carried out before developing a marketing mix, because many market forces bear upon it, including but not limited to the following:

- *Consumer attitudes and habits*: who consumes and why (the purchase motivation), purchase attitudes (what customers think of the product), consumer environment (social, legal, economic, political).

- *Other users such as industry buyers*: purchase motivation, industry practices (e.g., technical, operations processes), industry attitudes (e.g., quality, customer service), trends in procedures and methods.

- *Competition*: price as a determinant of competition, choice available to consumers, relative market position, intensity of direct competition, intensity of indirect competition, accepted competitive practices.

- *Government controls*: price controls, impact on competitive practices, controls on advertising and promotion.

4.1 PRODUCT

Products, formally defined, are the need-satisfying offerings of a company. Every company is selling satisfaction: the benefit that customers may desire and the need or want that they wish to fulfil. Note that when we define products from a marketing perspective, we usually do not talk about features, appearance, etc. but rather, we talk about the ultimate benefits that the product or service creates for the customer. An implication of this is that managers must be constantly concerned with product quality.

From a marketing perspective, quality is the product's ability to satisfy a customer's needs and requirements. For example, a product with more or better features is not a high-quality product if the features are not what the target market wants or needs. Remember that effective marketing strategy is reliant on consumer relevancy, as discussed in Part I.

A product can range from 100% emphasis on physical good (e.g., canned food) to 100% emphasis on service (e.g., legal advice). It can also be a combination of both (e.g., restaurant meals).

4.1.1. The hierarchy of product attributes

Marketers often try to differentiate their products in the minds of customers, so that specific and unique associations are made, which can make the product stand out from the competition. Products can usually have three layers, or dimensions. These are depicted in Figure 25 and are:

1. The *core product*: this is the undifferentiated product, or the core elements of the company's offering (for example, it refers to the generic product form, such as a basic TV box, or a car, etc with no added benefits). It represents a company's right to compete.

2. The *expected product*: when customers buy a car, they are usually not satisfied with a basic form of transportation (i.e., the core product). Nowadays, they expect a degree of comfort, a radio, reliability, and other features which are not strictly speaking necessary for the car to provide the core transportation benefit but are nonetheless expected by the customer. Hence, the expected layer is the means used by competing sellers to differentiate the product in the mind of customers (for example, the quality level, features, brand name, etc.). This is where some basic form of differentiation takes place.

3. The *augmented product*: some car makers, of course, go above and beyond in standing out from the competition. The augmented layer refers to the additional benefits that are provided to customers, in an attempt to increase the degree of differentiation between products. Elements of the product in this layer are usually unexpected but highly appreciated by the customer (for example, extra services, warranties, etc.). These elements are usually those that create an element of positive surprise and may therefore lead to exceeding customer expectations, and hence customer delight.

The more the product augmentations, the higher the degree of potential differentiation. But not all products need to be heavily augmented, of course, and not all customer segments require heavily augmented products.

Figure 25: The hierarchy of product attributes

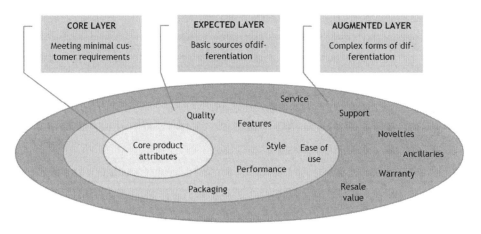

It is important to remember that too much differentiation can sometimes be harmful too. Many consumers think they want feature-loaded offerings when they are shopping, but once they start using the product they suffer "feature fatigue". They become overwhelmed by the product's complexity and annoyed by features they realise they don't want or need (and which they have paid for). The response: they return the item, take their business elsewhere and spread negative word-of-mouth. When thinking about product features and differentiation, it is good advice to do the following:

- *Assess complexity's costs:* Take a hard look at the level of complexity in the company's offerings and the difficulties it creates for the firm and the customers. A few years ago, Mercedes introduced many electronic features in their new models of cars, increasing the risk of parts malfunction, and making testing the electronic system more expensive. Many features were unnecessary but also annoyed customers (e.g., the key that saved the driver's settings was a good idea on paper, but it turned out to be problematic when husband and wife started sharing car keys!).

- *Balance initial sales against ease of use:* Identify the optimal number and type of features. Steer away from the extreme: too few features will make it hard to capture initial sales, while too many features will make the product hard to use. Compromise between the number of features and the cost of feature fatigue by finding the right balance of features against customer equity costs. For example, after considering the trade-off between initial sales of its vehicles and ease of use, Mercedes decided to remove more than 600 electronic functions from its cars.

- *Build simpler products:* Offer a wider assortment of simpler products targeted to narrower customer segments. For example, Xerox made very complex copy machines. After refinements and watching customers use the machines, they introduced the big green button that is now ubiquitous on every copier. Also, a company like Apple has maintained simplicity and focused on design, while its competitors strive to put everything into their products.

- *Help consumers decide:* Customer's decision-making is harder when they need to evaluate what features of a narrowly targeted product offering they actually need. Help customers by providing recommendations, trials, and other means to help them make an informed decision.

- *Design products that will do one thing very well:* Products that perform their central task (needed by customers) very well, will capture their owners' hearts. The Apple iPod is a perfect example of a simple product that did one thing well and was extremely successful as a consequence.

- *Use prototypes and product-in-use research:* To let consumers give usability its proper weight, it is not enough to ask consumers in market research to evaluate products without using them. Experimentation and even ethnography are important (as discussed in Part I).

The mobile telephony industry in the 1990s provides a very good example of what happens when complex differentiation backfires and when simple differentiation pays off. In the early 1990s, 6% of UK people owned a mobile phone. Analysts expected this to grow to 33% by 1995. Only two players were in the market: Vodafone and Cellnet. Two companies, Orange and One2One, were awarded identical simultaneous licences and had access to identical technology. In 1999, Deutsche Telekom bought One2One for £6.9b. Mannesmann bought Orange for £20b. Somehow, during the exact same period, one company (Orange) managed to build a lot more shareholder value than the other one (one2One). How did it do it?

The market offered great prospects for new players: exploit the overall market growth, attract new customers, and capture existing ones from the competition. With a level playing field, Orange's superior strategy and execution created almost 3 times as much shareholder value than One2One because it focused on doing one thing very well. By the time Orange and One2One launched their services, Vodafone and Cellnet were well established. However, subscribers had formed a negative image of the industry. The basic needs were simply not being met. Orange decided to offer what the market needed but was not getting: a simple, high-quality overall customer experience with good value for money. Orange realised that customers had fairly basic and well-defined needs: to get a signal, to be able to dial a number, to reach the intended number, to hold a clear conversation without being disconnected, to be charged a fair price for the call according to fair terms of contracts and to obtain helpful customer service when needed. Thus, Orange focused on delivering a high-quality overall customer experience with good value for money. It introduced rather simple innovations: per-second billing rather than rounding up to the minute (as was standard practice at the time), free itemised bills, a simple rate plan and fair contract, free insurance and good customer service. Orange was also the first mobile operator to put its logo on the phones it sold, increasing the visibility of the brand. These were not the product of cutting-edge and break-through R&D. They were just plain common sense. Orange simply took care of the basics that the others had neglected. It gave customers what really mattered. By doing this, Orange targeted the whole market with a generic benefit. Orange managed to meet the needs of the mass market by being the best at providing a benefit generic to the category.

One2One's differentiation strategy, in contrast, was not as successful. Since incumbents made most of their money from business customers, One2One saw an opportunity to differentiate itself by tapping into a gap in the market: it put a priority on big cities and offered free off-peak local calls. Having launched its services slightly earlier than Orange, One2One gained 64,000 subscribers in its first 6 months, twice as many as Orange in its first 6 months. But the differentiation strategy soon started to backfire; most of One2Ones customers were highly price sensitive. The free local calls deal meant that One2One's annual revenue per customer at £341 was lower than any competitor's and Orange led the industry, with annual revenue per customer of £442. Also, the off-peak calls overloaded the network, leading to poor quality, disconnections, busy networks and customer dissatisfaction.

The irony is that industry observers were initially concerned to see Orange head into a market as a 4th player with "no silver bullet". Not one element of its offer seemed proprietary or complex enough to provide a sustainable competitive advantage. Yet, two years later all competitors were copying several of its simple innovations. These were common-sense features, nothing extraordinary or very complex. They ensured that Orange continued to lead the market in providing the generic category benefits. Orange delivered the highest quality customer experience through its reliable service and value for money.

In short, Orange innovated in a simple way on dimensions that mattered to customers, and this led it to being voted "the most personable telecommunications company in the world". Orange delivered customer-focused differentiation. This is differentiation that matters. And the difference between Orange and One2One was worth £13 billion in shareholder value.

4.1.2. Product classification

Products tend to fit into one of two broad groups based on the type of customer that will use them: consumer products and industrial products. Consumer products are generally classified into convenience products (staples, impulse and emergency goods), shopping products (homogeneous or heterogeneous), specialty products and unsought products (either new or regularly unsought). Industrial products are classified into installations, accessory equipment, raw materials, components and professional services. These are summarised in Figure 26.

Figure 26: Classification of consumer and industrial products

CONSUMER PRODUCTS		INDUSTRIAL PRODUCTS
Meant for the final consumer, they are divided into classes depending on *how consumers think about and shop for products.*		Meant for use in producing other products, they are divided into classes depending on *how buyers think about products and how these will be used.*
Convenience products *Products customers need but are not willing to spend much time or effort shopping for.*	• Staples (e.g., canned food, milk, bread) • Impulse (e.g., ice cream, snacks) • Emergency (e.g. painkillers)	**Installations** *Usually consisting of buildings and fixed equipment.*
Shopping products *Products customers feel are worth the time and effort to compare with competing products.*	• Homogeneous (little difference among alternatives, e.g., refrigerators, white goods) • Heterogeneous (much difference between alternatives, e.g. clothes, shoes)	**Accessory equipment** *Products such as office equipment and mobile factory equipment.* **Raw materials** *Goods such as farm products or natural products, and goods often used to make other products.*
Specialty products *Products that are really wanted by the customer; the customer is willing to make a special effort to buy it. These products are not being compared with alternatives.*		**Components** *Parts and materials*
Unsought products *Products that potential customers don't search for as they do not yet want or know they can buy them.*	• New (need for product not strongly felt, e.g., a very new technology) • Regularly (aware of product but not interested, e.g., some insurance products, funeral services)	**Professional services** *Specialised services, for example to support a company's operation.*

It is important for marketers to understand exactly how their target markets classify the company's products. For example, for some consumers, coffee is an impulse product; they will consumer it on impulse when they see someone selling it, and they have limited brand loyalty. For others, it may be a shopping product; they like to buy and make their own coffee at home, and while they have some favourite brands, they may consider new ones every now and then and compare them. For other consumers, coffee is a specialty product; they have their favourite brand, and maybe even their preferred bar and barista, and they will not consider alternatives. Clearly, the implications for marketing strategy are significant, depending on how customers classify the product. The strategy must match the product classification from the point of view of the customer.

Packaging can also be a key element of a product, as it offers special opportunities to market the product, inform the customer and protect the product. To make the product more appealing to different target markets, variations in the packaging can be used. A specific package may have to be developed for each strategy. Packaging is also a key vehicle to communicate the brand's positioning in the market (for example, consider the packaging of exclusive brands compared to that of affordable brands).

4.1.3. Services as products

As already noted, companies do not compete only with physical products, but increasingly so with services. The marketing of services has been one of the fastest growing areas. Services have some characteristics that should be kept in mind and which complicate their marketing compared to physical products.

While physical products are high in search attributes (i.e., their quality can usually be ascertained with some confidence prior to purchase), services are typically high in experience or credence attributes. In other words, their quality can only be assessed after the purchase (e.g., a cruise or a flight), or in some cases it cannot be assessed with certainty even after the purchase and experience (e.g., consulting services and medical advice).

The primary unique features of services are the following:

- *Intangibility*: services cannot be touched and felt. The challenge for service marketers is therefore to reduce customer's perceived risk and provide some physical or visual evidence, such as logos etc., to help customers assess service quality.

- *Simultaneous production*: services are typically provided in the customer's presence and consumed simultaneously to production. They are usually sold first and then produced. For example, when a customer gets a haircut, the customer must be in the salon for the service delivery to take place. This obviously has implications in terms of managing the face-to-face contact with the producer (which usually does not happen when the product is fully tangible).

- *Perishability*: unlike physical products, services cannot be stored and inventoried. If a plane seat is not sold or a hotel room not filled, it cannot be offered to the market again at a later stage; it is lost. For this reason, it may be difficult to achieve economies of scale when the product emphasis is on service. And there are also significant implications in terms of managing seasonality and fluctuations in demand and supply.

- *Variability*: a service is performed anew for each customer. Therefore, there is some risk involved for the consumer, due to what marketers call a "leap of faith" (i.e., we must believe that the service provider will do a good job, as we cannot assess the quality prior to consumption). Variability also means that different customers might have different experiences and opinions of a service provider. It might also mean that the same customer might face significant variations in the quality of the service from one day to another. For example, a customer buying a can of Coca-Cola can expect consistent quality every time. But a customer buying a haircut may be satisfied on one occasion, but dissatisfied the next, even if the hairdresser is the same. Variability can happen from service provider to service provider, from user to user, and from time to time.

For these reasons, services need some additional attention beyond the traditional 4 Ps. We deal with these peculiarities of services by extending the marketing mix and adding an extra 3 Ps:

1. *Physical evidence*: this is the provision of something physical or tangible in what is otherwise an intangible service. For example, doctors' offices usually try to be tidy and clean, with University qualifications neatly displayed on the wall, along with awards and other clues that try to reduce perceived intangibility by focusing attention on some tangibles.

2. *People (or Participants)*: because of the factors discussed above, and in particular service variability, effective training of service providers is essential. Every encounter is a "moment of truth", or an opportunity to satisfy or dissatisfy a customer. Also, in service provision, other customers might affect one customers' experience

(e.g., queuing at a bank teller, or shopping in a retail environment), so these should be managed effectively as well.

3. *Process*: another way to reduce variability is by standardising processes. In other words, we can systematise and standardise the way in which the service is delivered, so that customers always have the same experience. For example, the way in which McDonald's serves its customers is based on a systematic process, which ensures that customers all around the world experience pretty much the same level of service.

We have already hinted to the fact that service quality is typically more difficult to assess than the quality of physical products. This is primarily due to intangibility (i.e., you cannot touch and feel services). For this reason, marketing researchers have been studying the determinants of service quality, and evidence suggests that companies that provide superior service quality usually perform well along the following 5 dimensions:

1. *Reliability*: reliable service, people, etc.

2. *Responsiveness*: adapt the service delivery to customer requirements, be responsive.

3. *Assurance*: make the customer feel safe, comfortable and confident about the service.

4. *Empathy*: not only understanding customers, but actually feeling what they feel.

5. *Tangibles*: increase physical evidence, ensure that anything that is tangible about the service is as good as it can possibly be.

4.1.4. Management of product life cycles

An important part of marketing is to manage products over time and, eventually, plan for their successors. Understanding the stages that a product goes through, from beginning to end, is an imperative for marketers wishing to manage for the long term.

The Product Life Cycle (PLC) is a model that describes the stages a new product goes through from beginning to end. The model is useful to marketers, because different marketing mixes and strategies are required as the product moves through its cycle. This is because, for example, customers' attitudes and needs may change, the company may aim at a different target market at different stages, or competition may vary. In fact, two of the main forces shaping the PLC are consumer behaviour (e.g., the rate of adoption) and competitive actions.

Figure 27: The Product Life Cycle

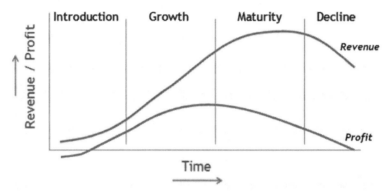

The PLC model plots total sales revenue and total profit in an industry. Each of the four stages has a different level of total sales of product by all industry players. Also, profitability changes over time. Note that industry profits start to decline while industry sales are still rising; this is primarily because of more intense competition, pressure on prices, and changing consumer preferences.

Introduction is typically marked by loss and the company needs to develop the entire marketing mix. Building awareness, stablishing value and a sales volume focus are paramount. Growth sees an increase in product variety, but monopoly profits start to attract new entrants. In this stage the company may wish to expand distribution, differentiate, implement persuasive marketing activities and enter new markets. Maturity starts when there is market saturation and is typically marked by intense competition. Prices tend to fall, and the industry may become more commoditised. In this stage, persuasive, direct marketing communication is common and there is a shift from a sales to a productivity focus. Finally, in the decline stage of the PLC the company may consider rationalising product lines, focusing on profitable niches and look for new products to replace the old ones. Harvest and divest strategic objectives are the norm in the stage of the PLC.

While the PLC model does not really have predictive power (at best it can give you an indication of the stage in which your product is currently), it is useful because it suggests a number of strategic implications depending

106

on the stage in which your product finds itself. Some of these implications are outlined in Figure 28.

Figure 28: The PLC and implications for marketing

PLC STAGE	CHARACTERISTICS AND IMPLICATIONS FOR MARKETING
1. INTRODUCTION	• Sales are low as the new product is introduced into the market. • Usually marked by loss, as relatively large costs are incurred on promotion, product and place development. • Little competition is present. • Firms need to be flexible, in order to adapt to meet the emerging needs of consumers. • **Major marketing activities: (1) build brand awareness and (2) establish distribution.**
2. GROWTH	• Industry sales are growing fast, but industry profits rise and then start falling. • New competitors start entering the market, resulting in product variety and monopolistic competition. • Monopoly profits attract new entrants (this is the time of highest profits in the industry). • **Major marketing activities: (1) expand distribution, (2) differentiate products (add new models etc.), (3) improve the product (e.g. quality, features) and (4) enter new markets.** • If a product can't be differentiated, then price is the only basis for competition.
3. MATURITY	• Industry sales level off and competition becomes more intense. There is over capacity. • Prices are low, promotion is high and there are difficulties in the management of the product. • Curves become increasingly elastic, as little differentiation is perceived by customer. • **Major marketing activities: (1) attract existing customers rather than new ones (i.e. focus on winning competitors' customers, for example, through persuasive promotion).**

4. DECLINE

- New products replace the old ones.

- Profits can still be made (e.g. if not much competition is left).

- **Major marketing activities: (1) withdraw from the market, (2) rationalise product line, (3) focus on remaining pockets of demand.**

It is important to note that the PLC describes industry sales and profits for a product within a particular market. The sales and profits of an individual product or brand may not, and often do not, follow the typical life cycle pattern. They may vary up and down throughout the life cycle, sometimes moving in the opposite direction of total industry sales and profits. Moreover, a product may be in different life cycle stages in different markets. Again, the duration and length of each stage will depend mainly on the level and type of competition and consumer behaviour.

The PLC model can be applied in at least three different product areas:

1. *Product categories* (e.g., milk): it is at this level that we tend to see the longest PLCs with well-defined S-shaped curves.

2. *Product forms* (e.g., low fat milk): at this level we tend see fairly stable PLCs, but shorter than in product categories.

3. *Brands* (e.g., Nestle low-fat milk): at this level we tend to see the shortest PLC curves. Nowadays many brands take a mere 3 years to progress through the entire PLC.

In general, product life cycles are becoming shorter and shorter. This is partly due to rapid technological changes. As a consequence, companies must develop new products continually and they must try to have marketing mixes that will make the most of the market growth stage when profits are highest.

Clearly, the sales of some products are heavily influenced by fashion (currently accepted or popular style) or fads (ideas that are fashionable only to a certain group of enthusiasts and for a short period of time). In these cases, a product's curve tends to peak quickly but usually drop off fast.

The correct strategy to adopt depends on how fast the product is likely to move through the life cycle or how quickly the new idea will be accepted by customers, as well as how quickly competitors will follow with their own versions of the product.

It should be noted that at the decline stage, a company should not passively accept lower sales of a product. There are other options. A company could improve its product or develop an innovative new product for the same market. It could also develop a strategy for its product targeted at a new market. Alternatively, it could withdraw the product before it completes the cycle and refocus its resources on better opportunities. The wisest move may often be to slowly and gradually phase the product out of the market.

4.1.5. Factors affecting product diffusion

The question of what determines the success of a new product (e.g., what makes it go quickly from introduction to growth) or its failure (e.g., why it does not make it past the introductory stage) has puzzled researchers for a long time. Some products tend to have a long introductory stage and then disappear slowly. Others seem to break through the clutter at some point and become runaway successes, seemingly almost overnight.

At least two factors are important is shaping the PLC. The first one is competitions. The curve will have a different shape depending on whether competitors respond or not, and if so, how quickly.

Second, consumer behaviour can determine the success of an innovation. There is a chasm between the early adopters of a product (e.g., technology enthusiasts and visionaries) and the early majority (the pragmatists). Products can become successful when they cross this chasm, and it is a good idea to focus on one group of customers at a time, using each group as a base for marketing to the next group. In fact, later adopters will often look at earlier adopters, who influence their behaviour, so targeted growth that avoids premature scaling is often desirable.

Research has shown that at least five factors affect the odds that an innovation will penetrate a market successfully. These are:

1. *Relative advantage:* the degree to which a product is perceived to be superior to existing products it is designed to replace (e.g., computers took off quickly because of their superiority over manually kept records).

2. *Compatibility:* the degree to which the product matches the values and lifestyle of the potential purchaser (e.g., the use of a keyboard with the same layout as a typewriter made the take-off of home PCs quicker, despite the fact that the original QWERTY layout was not necessarily the best for quick typing).

3. *Complexity:* the degree of difficulty in using the product (e.g., products that are simpler to use will tend to take off more quickly).

4. *Divisibility:* the opportunity to try the product on a limited basis (e.g., software companies let consumers install and use the product for a certain period before asking for payment – this encourages trial and improves the likelihood of adoption).

5. *Communicability:* the degree to which the product's performance capabilities are evident in use (e.g., any benefit and feature need to be clearly communicated to the customer – they need to be visible when the customer uses the product).

4.1.6. The adoption process

When consumers face a new product concept, their previous experience may not be relevant to the problem-solving situation at hand. These situations involve a new adoption process, that is, a number of steps individuals go through on the way to accepting or rejecting a new idea. In the adoption process, a customer moves through some fairly distinct phases:

1. Awareness (coming to know about the existence of the product)

2. Interest (gathering of more information about the product)

3. Evaluation (giving the product a mental trial)

4. Trial (the consumer may adopt the product for trial, if feasible)

5. Decision (the consumer decides whether to adopt or reject the product)

6. Confirmation (the consumer compares outcomes with initial expectations to determine whether he/she is satisfied)

Fundamentally, the role of the marketer is to speed up and simplify this process as much as possible. It is important to know the exact steps that consumers go through in adopting an innovation, so that the correct information may be provided to them at the right time, in the right quantity, and in the right places.

Also, some segments of the market may be in different stages of adoption, thus requiring different strategies. In fact, knowing the timing of adoption of different customer groups can be essential to the success of a marketing strategy.

The adoption curve model was devised based on research on how markets accept new ideas. This shows when different adopter groups accept new ideas, emphasising the relationship between groups and showing that some act as leaders in accepting a new idea. The model is depicted in Figure 29.

Figure 29: The Adoption Curve

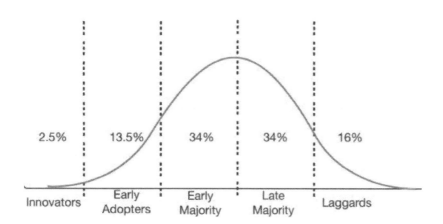

Adopter categories are used to classify individuals based on innovativeness. There are five categories of adopters: innovators (which make up a small 2.5% of adopters), early adopters (making up 13.5% of adopters), early majority (34%), late majority (34%), and laggards (16%). The characteristics of each adopter group are summarized in Figure 30.

Figure 30: Characteristics of adopter groups

INNOVATORS	• Innovators are the first individuals to adopt an innovation and make up 2.5% of all adopters of an innovation. • Innovators are willing to take risks, are typically youngest in age, have the highest social class, have great financial liquidity, are very social and have closest contact to scientific sources and interaction with other innovators. • Risk tolerance has them adopting technologies which may ultimately fail. Financial resources help absorb these failures. • Innovators exercise influence on early adopters, and therefore, can be used cleverly by marketers. An example is bloggers and other influencers who are used by companies to test their products, review them, and encourage others to try them.
EARLY ADOPTERS	• This is the second fastest category of individuals who adopt an innovation and constitute 13.5% of all adopters. • These individuals also enjoy a very high degree of opinion leadership among the other adopter categories (i.e., they will influence others to buy a product). • Early Adopters are typically younger in age, have a higher social status, have more financial resources, advanced education, and are more socially forward than late adopters. • They are more discrete in adoption choices than innovators.
EARLY MAJORITY	• Early Majority make up a large share (34%) of total adopters of an innovation. • Consumers in the Early Majority category take a varying degree of time to adopt an innovation, which is much longer than the time taken by Early Adopters and Innovators. • Early Majority tend to be slower in the adoption process, have above-average social status, contact with Early Adopters, and seldom hold positions of opinion leadership among peers.
LATE MAJORITY	• Like Early Majority, this group constitutes a dominant adopter group, as it is made up of 34% of all adopters. • The Late Majority accepts an innovation after the average consumer has adopted it. For that reason, the term "late" is used.

	• These individuals approach an innovation with a high degree of scepticism and tend to adopt it after the majority of society has already adopted it.
	• Late Majority are typically sceptical about an innovation, have below average social status, very little financial liquidity, limited contact with others in Late Majority and Early Majority, and very little opinion leadership.
LAGGARDS	• This group is made up of 16% of total adopters of an innovation. Individuals in this category are the last to adopt an innovation.
	• Laggards exhibit limited opinion leadership. They have virtually no influence on others.
	• Laggards have a resistance to change-agents and are usually advanced in age.
	• Laggards typically tend to be focused on "traditions", are likely to have low social status, low financial liquidity, and being the oldest of all other adopters, are in contact with only family and close friends.

Marketers should pay attention to the diffusion process, as it determines the success and failure of new products introduced in the market. Usually, the objective is to obtain the largest amount of adoption within the shortest period of time.

The rate of adoption is defined as the relative speed with which members of the market adopt an innovation. It is usually measured by the length of time required for a certain percentage of the members of that market to adopt the innovation. The rates of adoption for innovations are determined by that individual's adopter category (e.g., innovator, early adopter, etc.). Generally, those consumers who accept and use an innovation first have a shorter adoption period (or adoption process) than those consumers who are later in adoption. Innovation can reach a critical mass during the rate of adoption. When a product crosses this point, which is usually between the introduction and growth stages of the PLC, the product has crossed the chasm. At that point, an increasingly larger number of customers are buying the product, and adoption of the innovation becomes self-sustaining. Innovators play a key role in ensuring that a product reaches critical mass. It is often their word of mouth, referrals, and influence on less risk-taking consumers that help push a product further down the adoption curve.

4.2 Marketing Communications

One of the key tasks of marketing is to communicate with the market in order to build interest in a product, obtain trial, speed up adoption, etc. This element of the marketing mix is very important because while a product can be high in value, that value is useless until it is actually perceived by the customers.

Figure 31: The communication process

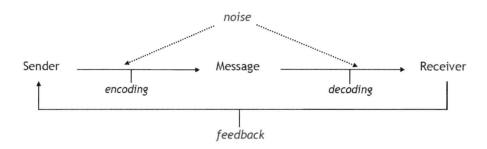

To understand how marketing communication works, it is useful to consider some fundamental concepts of communication. The diagram in Figure 31 outlines a model of the communication process. Pretty much all communication works like this, and from a marketing point of view, there are a number of key points to consider with regard to the communication model. The model teaches us the following important implications: First, the sender must always know exactly what audiences he/she wants to reach, and what responses are desired. Second, the sender must understand how the target audience will decode the message. Third, the message must be transmitted through efficient media, which should reach the target audience and allow for effective communication. Receivers attach different value to different channels. Fourth, the sender must develop feedback channels so that he/she can have the receiver's response to the message and gauge whether the communication process has been effective. Finally, different audiences may decode and hence interpret the same message in different ways.

These are important points to remember, because promotion can be wasted if it does not communicate effectively. There are many reasons why a promotional message can be misunderstood or not heard at all. The communication process model helps us understand this. Sometimes an advertisement fails because it does not reach the intended audience (e.g., a gardening accessories brand that uses mass media channels like TV—therefore reaching millions of people with no garden—instead of more targeted channels like gardening magazines), or because it is not encoded and/or decoded correctly (e.g., when Electrolux used the slogan "nothing sucks like an Electrolux" vacuum cleaner, the audience assumed the product was poor, instead of having superior suction). Sometimes no feedback channels are developed to study the reaction of customers to the message, or there is simply too much noise (e.g., competitors' advertisements create clutter and make it difficult for our message to work).

4.2.1. Steps in developing marketing communications

To develop a marketing communications strategy, it is useful to follow a number of steps. These are the typical stages of an effective communications strategy:

1. *Identify the target audience*

   - This has to be done carefully, through effective market research, and by taking all segmentation issues into consideration.

2. *Determine the communication objectives*

   - Marketers need to be clear about the objectives of their communications strategy. At the most fundamental level, communications can be either strategic (e.g., to build a brand in the long term) or tactical (e.g., to stimulate immediate demand for a product). Therefore, a communication strategy may be employed to achieve the following objectives:

     - Help introduce new products.
     - Aid the positioning strategy through informing and persuading.
     - Help obtain distribution (e.g., via a push strategy, which involves promoting to channel members in order to convince them to encourage consumers to buy the product, or via a pull strategy, by promoting to final consumers in order to motivate them to seek the product from channel members).
     - Arouse interest and prepare the way for an aggressive selling effort.

- Get immediate buying action, or confirm the purchase decisions of buyers (i.e., remind customers who have already bought the product that it was a good decision).

3. *Design the message*

- The next step involves choosing the type of advertising to be employed (for example, will it promote the corporate brand or a specific product? Will it compare the product to competing products? Will it build primary demand?)

- In designing the message, one should consider the AIDA model (this is discussed in more detail later in section 4.3.2), message content, structure, format and source.

4. *Select the communications channel*

- This choice can be very broad and fundamentally involves choosing between personal channels (e.g., face to face, telephone or mail) and non-personal channels (e.g., media, events).

5. *Decide on the promotional mix*

- Marketers can use many different methods to promote products. The choice often falls among methods such as advertising, sales promotion, personal selling and publicity. These are discussed in the next section.

- When devising the promotional mix, the type of product market shall be considered. For example, should the communications strategy target final consumers (so the emphasis may be more on advertising, publicity and sales promotion) or industrial buyers (so the emphasis might be more on personal selling).

- One should also take into account consumer's involvement level and the complexity of the product. For low involvement and simple products, advertising can be an effective choice. For high involvement products, personal selling may be preferred.

- One could also consult the Product Life Cycle when devising the promotional mix. For instance, innovators and early adopters can be addressed with a targeted advertisement in the early stages, whereas consumers in the majority and

116

growth stages can be reached through mass-marketing methods.

- Choosing between a push or a pull strategy is also important. That is, will the business promote to channel members to ensure the latter actively sell its products to end consumers, or should it promote to the final customers themselves, so they will look for the products wherever they are made available?

6. *Establish the budget*

- An important step of the marketing communications process is to set the budget. There are many ways in which this may be done, for example through the percentage of sales method (i.e., take a certain percentage of total revenue for marketing communications spending), the affordability method (i.e., spend whatever you can afford), and the competitive parity method (i.e., spend the same amount as the most direct competitors).

7. *Measure results*

- Finally, it is important to compare the outcomes of the marketing communications strategy versus the objectives that were set initially. Were the objectives achieved? Why or why not? And what kind of adjustments may be needed to the communications strategy?

4.2.2. Promotional methods, objectives and the adoption process

Promotion is fundamentally any kind of persuasive communication, and it can take many different forms. A company can choose from several methods as part of its promotional mix, including the following:

1. *Personal selling*: direct (usually spoken) communication between sellers and potential customers. This is typically done in person through the use of salespeople, but sometimes also over the phone, internet, etc.

2. *Advertising*: any paid form of non-personal communication about ideas, goods or services by an identified source, for example on TV and radio, in cinemas, or through the use of display banners and videos online.

3. *Publicity*: any unpaid form of non-personal communication about idea, goods or services. Reviews of a firm's product in the press or by a blogger, for example, fall within this category.

4. *Public relations*: communication aimed at improving the attitudes of various identified groups toward the company or its products, for example, using the company website.

5. *Sales promotion*: all promotional activities, excluding advertising, publicity or public relations and personal selling, which aim to stimulate interest, trial or purchase by final consumers or intermediaries (e.g., vouchers, competitions, etc.).

Choosing which methods to use depends on the promotional objectives of the company, the overall objective being to influence consumer behaviour. Marketers are interested in either reinforcing present attitudes that might lead to favourable behaviour, or in changing the attitudes and behaviour of the company's target market. Promotional strategies must of course take into account the competition, consumer behaviour, government regulations and other environmental factors and trends.

There are three basic promotion objectives, which should be used at different points in time (but which may also be combined), depending on the stage of the adoption process of the target market:

1. *Inform*: communication may be needed to inform customers of a product, its features, etc. This is typically the main objective when a product is first introduced in the market.

2. *Persuade*: communication can attempt to shape customers' perceptions or behaviour directly. Here marketing communication is more persuasive and is designed to affect the customer's decision-making process. This is typical when customers face a number of choices and marketers want their product to stand out.

3. *Remind*: communication can be used to keep a brand alive in the mind of the customer, to increase the odds of repurchase. This is typically used when customers are already aware of the product or service and may even have already purchased it before. Reminding customers of a brand even after they have already bought it, can increase the chance of repeat business and loyalty.

All marketing communication has one of the above objectives, or a combination of them. The important thing to note is that marketers need to be clear about their communication objectives, which will be heavily influenced by the customer's position in the adoption process. The adoption process can be divided into 6 stages:

1. Awareness (the customer finds out about the product)
2. Interest (the customer becomes attracted to the product and considers purchasing it to satisfy a need)
3. Evaluation (the customer starts considering alternative options/brands that may satisfy the need)
4. Trial (the customer tries a specific product or brand)
5. Decision (the customer decides whether to buy it or not)
6. Confirmation (if the product is bought, the customer compares the outcome to the expectation to determine the level of satisfaction with it and whether a good decision was made)

The purpose of marketing communications is fundamentally to move the customer through this adoption process. In a way, a marketer should try and take the customer by the hand at the awareness stage, and help them all the way through to confirmation, providing the correct information, at the best time and best place.

Thus, it makes sense to start by informing, then persuading, and eventually reminding. First, when a customer develops a need, he or she needs to become aware of alternative options that can satisfy that need. Informing is therefore key. Interest may then develop in a particular set of options, which are then evaluated. Once the customer identifies a product or service that seems to meet his or her needs, trial is the next natural step. Communication should therefore become more persuasive, and not just informative. This is followed by a decision to purchase the product or not, and eventually, a confirmation of whether that decision was correct (e.g., by comparing the outcome with the initial expectations). Reminder advertising becomes critical here to reinforce the customer's decision and increase the chances he/she may return.

So, in short, informing and persuading may be required to affect the potential customer's knowledge and attitudes about the product, and then bring about its adoption. Later promotion can simply remind the customer about the favourable experience and confirm the adoption decision.

It is important to know at what stage of the adoption process each target market is, as this will dictate what objectives to set for the communications strategy. It's important to remember that in the end, one of the key purposes of marketing is to speed up the decision-making process of customers and improve the rate at which they adopt a company's products and services.

To identify and allocate communications objectives, marketers can also use a tool called the "AIDA model". The model describes four promotional tasks:

1. To get *attention (A)*
2. To hold *interest (I)*
3. To arouse *desire (D)*
4. To obtain *action (A)*

Obtaining consumer's attention is key in making them aware of the firm's offering. Holding interest gives the communication a chance to develop the consumer's interest in the product. Arousing desire affects the evaluation process, ideally by building preference. Obtaining action includes gaining trial, which may then lead to a further purchase decision. Continuing promotion is necessary to confirm the decision and encourage additional purchases.

Figure 32 depicts the relationship between promotion objectives, adoption process and the AIDA model.

The key principle here is that the promotion objectives will have to match the stage of the adoption process in which the target market is positioned. Similarly, the AIDA model suggests that different tasks will be most relevant according to the stage of adoption. For example, a customer who is only just starting to find out about a company's product should be targeted with informative promotion, and the key task of that promotion will be to first get the customer's attention, and then hold his or her interest. In this case, teaser advertising with an information message might do the job. In contrast, if the customer knows about the product but has not yet tried it, a marketer may wish to use very persuasive communication designed to arouse desire in the product. A sales promotion with some kind of incentive may be useful here. And a customer who has already purchased a product before only needs to be reminded of the product, so that the same purchase decision may be made again. The associated task is to obtain action, i.e., a purchase. In this case, a special offer to returning customers may be employed for this purpose.

Figure 32: Promotion objectives, the adoption process and the AIDA model

PROMOTION OBJECTIVES	ADOPTION PROCESS	AIDA MODEL
Informing	Awareness	Attention
	Interest	Interest
	Evaluation	
Persuading	Trial	Desire
Reminding	Decision	
	Confirmation	Action

In short, marketers need to ask themselves: at what stage of the adoption process is my target market? This may vary according to each segment, of course. Depending on the adoption stage, the marketer is then able to select a promotion objective and associated tasks (AIDA model). These decisions allow companies to focus their communications strategy so that it is most efficient and effective.

There should also be variations in promotions for different adopter groups. Early adopters are probably the most likely to have contact with salespeople, and the acceptance of this group is very important in reaching the next group, since the early majority looks to the early adopters for guidance. The early majority has a great deal of contact with mass media, salespeople, and early adopters who act as opinion leaders. In contrast, the late majority makes little use of marketing sources of information such as mass media or salespeople. They tend to be oriented more to other late adopters rather than outside sources (which they do not trust). Finally, sometimes it may not be worthwhile to target laggards at all.

It is important to remember that the communications strategy should generally need to change depending on the stage of the PLC. For example, over the life of a product or service, communications might need to change as set out in Figure 33 below.

Figure 33: Marketing communications and the PLC

Introduction	Growth	Maturity	Decline
Build primary demand.	Build selective demand.	Even more persuasive.	Promotion is more targeted.
Inform.	Persuade.	Advertising and sales promotion dominate for consumer products. Reminder advertising for strong brands.	Promotion expenses decrease or increase if company wants to slow down cycle.

Time

4.2.3. Advertising

Mass communication, which includes advertising, public relations and publicity, makes widespread distribution possible; for example, advertising can reach large numbers of potential customers simultaneously. It can inform and persuade customers and help position a company's marketing mix as one that meets customers' needs.

In relation to advertising, managers must decide which type to employ, as each form of advertising has its strengths and limitations.

The advertising objectives largely determine which of the two basic types of advertising to use: product advertising (advertising that tries to sell a specific product) or institutional advertising (advertising that tries to promote an organisation's image, reputation or ideas, rather than a specific product).

There are 4 main types of product advertising:

1. *Pioneering advertising*: this type of advertising aims to develop primary demand for a product category rather than for a specific brand. This is the kind of advertising typically used by first movers.
2. *Competitive advertising*: attempts to develop selective demand for a specific brand. It aims at achieving immediate buying action. This is the most popular type of advertising,
3. *Comparative advertising*: this type of advertising is more aggressive and involves making specific brand comparisons using actual

product or brand names (e.g., Coke arguing in its own advertisements that it is better than Pepsi). It is not permitted in numerous countries.

4. *Reminder advertising*: it tries to keep the product's name in the public's mind. It may be useful when the product has already achieved a degree of brand preference or insistence.

In the same way as the overall communication strategy needs to adapt over the life of a product and depending on the customers' stage of adoption, advertising type will also change as customers proceed through their adoption stages. Figure 34 summarises some of the options that advertisers use to keep up with the stages of adoption.

Figure 34: Examples of different types of advertising over the adoption process stages

Awareness	→ Interest	→ Evaluation & trial	→ Decision	→ Confirmation
Teaser campaigns, pioneering ads, jingles and slogans. Announcements.	Informative or descriptive ads. Image/celebrity ads. Demonstration of benefits.	Competitive ads. Persuasive ads. Comparative ads. Testimonials.	Direct-action retail ads. Point-of-purchase ads. Price deal offers.	Reminder ads. Informative 'why' ads.

In many countries, yearly spending on online marketing has already overtaken spending on any other communications tools. In the UK this already happened around 2012, when more than a quarter of communications spending was online. This was higher than TV (24%), press (18%), direct mail (10%) and classifieds (8%). Companies have realised the potential of the internet to communicate with their customers.

There are many tools available to online marketers. The most popular ones may be categorised into five groups:

1. *Display advertising*: Online display advertising is the cornerstone of digital marketing. It involves showing banners and other display tools on internet pages. Display advertising has been around since the mid-1990s and in a country like the UK, for example, it accounts for about a billion of spending, which is by far the largest amount of online marketing spending. Online displays are useful

123

primarily to deliver brand messages, to immerse consumers with interactive experiences and to generate a direct and measurable response from consumers.

2. *Games advertising*: This is one of the most dynamic and fast-growing disciplines within the online landscape. It involves placing advertising within a gaming environment and/or using bespoke games to promote a product or service. Advertisers benefit from the growing audience of highly engaged consumers.

3. *Mobile marketing*: This is becoming more and more the central focus of many media plans. As awareness and understanding grows, advertisers are increasingly embracing the potential of mobile. Mobile advertising is growing dramatically, especially since mobile internet has become ubiquitous and the processing power of devices has improved. The range of advertisers using mobile to benefit their brands is also becoming broader as more mainstream brands from sectors such as finance and consumer goods are investing on mobile.

4. *Video marketing*: Online video advertising (placing video clips with commercial messages online whether on the company website, a site like YouTube, etc.) is also a growing advertising format and is becoming an important way to build brands. There has been an explosive growth in spending of nearly 100% year on year in many developed countries.

5. *Social media marketing*: Finally, social media marketing has become a very widely used tool to communicate with customers. Social networks now account for a quarter of the time that consumers spend online in countries like the UK and the USA. Social media encompasses a vast range of activities, including social networking, blogging, word of mouth, content dissemination, user generated content, crowd sourcing, interactive advertising and more. There are three areas of social media: (1) "Paid", for instance adverts on social networks; (2) "Earned", for instance genuine product or service reviews by bloggers, and (3) "Owned", for instance as a brand's official page in a social network.

Maintaining an active social media presence is often seen as an alternative to traditional advertising and as a means of achieving brand awareness. This is particularly true when advertising and online word of mouth compete for shrinking marketing budgets. However, evidence suggests that advertising and fostering word of mouth on social media are not substitutable. Instead, they are complimentary. Thus, attention should be paid to both traditional means of communicating with customers, and online social media tools. For example, while word of mouth through social media can be effective in driving sales quickly in an unobtrusive way, traditional marketing communications can still be important to have more control over the message, the channel and the frequency of communication, as well as to build brand value and reduce price sensitivity in the long term.

4.2.4. The impact of media convergence on advertising

Media convergence (i.e., the ability to deliver different media channels via one digital platform) is creating a new media age. In the past, different platforms distributed the broadcast media (radio, television, internet). Nevertheless, with the rise of content marketing, changes and complexity are emerging in the media business model.

Even prior to the advent of media convergence, the efficiency of the traditional media business model was already declining due to an over-supply and commoditisation of media content, and a decline of advertising effectiveness. The internet accelerated the commoditisation of media, by giving consumers free access to up-to-date content, and media channels today are struggling to determine new viable revenue streams. And advertising, which has already been among the most inefficient means of communication in terms of its ability to target specific customer groups, is now suffering from increased audience fragmentation and advertising clutter.

The traditional business model was founded on the media owner's ability to consolidate audiences. The larger the audience, the larger the premium paid for the media. For example, primetime TV typically has a Cost per Thousand (a common media metric that identifies the price of reaching one thousand individuals within a stated target group) of about four times that of an average daytime spot. Large audience sizes are declining as more channels and vehicles emerge and audiences are spread more thinly across different media opportunities. This means that the advertiser is in a difficult situation, arising from the problems with reaching a targeted audience in a coordinated fashion. The media owner also finds itself in a difficulty, as is present with fewer opportunities of charging higher prices to reach a targeted audience, reducing its' revenues.

The amount of advertising carried by media owners has increased significantly in recent years, as has the proliferation of touchpoints: advertising is gaining access to vehicles such as billboards in unexpected places, promotions in the street, or advertising on mobile phones. Evidence suggests that advertising spending is increasing for all touchpoints, and particularly for digital. Some sources suggest that consumers see between 1000 and 3000 commercial messages per day, with many of them feeling overwhelmed. Furthermore, the rate of decay (i.e., forgetting a particular advertisement) tends to increase as consumers are exposed to a higher volume of advertising. Therefore, consumers are becoming increasingly more desensitised to advertising, with both conscious and sub-conscious behavioural outcomes (e.g., by 'zapping', leaving the room, or simply ignoring the message).

The new media age has enabled consumers to choose the content they want to consume, the way and time they want it, often for free or without advertisements. This development has several implications:

1. *Democratization of content*: Users can upload entertainment content on the internet easily for public access. The sharing of professional content is arguably the single largest threat to the media industry, and peer-to-peer sharing is free of charge and free of advertising, which means content producers are not remunerated. Content, it appears, is increasingly being made 'for the people, by the people'. It is now possible to host and offer an almost limitless array of content, which ensures almost every consumer need is met. The provision of a wealth of specialist products with small individual sales but large collective profit potential is now economically viable, and media owners can now provide mechanisms for consumers to find this content.

2. *User-generated content*: Media convergence has also empowered users to produce and distribute their own content. Production costs are falling, due for example to digitalisation, and the internet provides an excellent open-source distribution platform to a large audience via the internet. User-generated content gives scope for co-creation in the form of blogging and, more recently, the rise of amateur content that is distributed via television. Also, user-generated content can act as a powerful marketing tool not

only to engage consumers, but ultimately also to shape profession-
ally produced content.

3. *Personalization of schedules:* It is now possible for consumers to
watch what they want and when they want it, via on-demand content or search content. Personal Video Recorders already enabled
the consumer to individualise their schedules by recording large
quantities of content and enabling consumers to skip over advertising. Now content has become more mobile and place-shifting
technology enables consumers to remotely view content from
their devices.

4. *Social networking and virtual reality:* The internet has developed
into a tool that enables users to engage with one another, known
as peer to peer (P2P) engagement, which has brought about the
existence of digital communities. Social networking is no longer
for niche 'technophiles', but it can be applied to the broader market. The advertising potential is significant, as long as the users
do not feel that the community is becoming too commercial, so it
must be done with discretion and not be too overt. Firms can find
opportunities in upselling and cross promoting content, as well as
can trigger consumer engagement using their brand name in innovative ways.

5. *Divergence of consumer groups:* A new generation of media consumers has emerged, comprised of media literate and tech savvy
consumers. Two adopter groups may be identified. First, 'actives',
or early adopters, who rely upon technology not only for entertainment, but as a support for their social network. They are characterised by short attention spans and engage with multiple media
channels simultaneously. They are more proactive in their content
choice, seeking out specific programming, gaming or P2P content.
This is also known as 'lean-forward' engagement. The second
group, 'passives', or late adopters, are individuals who are content with their current entertainment experience. This group is
likely to keep the TV as the centrepiece to their entertainment
experience, letting the schedulers meet their entertainment
needs. This is known as 'lean-back engagement'. IBM has identified a 'generational chasm' between the two segments. The youth
market sees a greater adoption of emerging technology. As the
youth matures, they continue to observe their media consumption

habits, introducing their behaviour in the mass market. A new youth generation also emerges, giving rise to new early adopters. As a result, the generational chasm will close as media convergence becomes a mass market phenomenon. This will ultimately result in the 'new' and the 'old' media world's co-existence, and eventually, their merging. Even though 'lean-forward' engagement will continue to grow, TV will still remain a leading leisure time activity. It is also likely that consumers will continue to have a balanced schedule of activity. They will have active (lean forward) moments when users seek specific content and lean-back moments when they want a more passive experience.

As consumers are empowered to consume any media they want, when, were and how they want it, audiences have become increasingly fragmented. Furthermore, customers can avoid the advertising messages as a whole. Because advertising is such a significant part of the media owner's revenue stream, it is no wonder that the media industry is in a mild state of panic. Media owners need, firstly, to try to re-invigorate advertising to ensure it is still relevant in the new era. Secondly, the decline of the model highlights the need to diversify into other revenue streams.

4.2.5. Defeating customer apathy

The discussion above suggests that marketers nowadays face several challenges in reaching customers and ensuring that their message resonates with them. In addition to the aforementioned issues, customers are also becoming increasingly apathetic. They are less and less likely to pay attention to commercial messages, they are not as interested in brands as marketers often like to assume, they have no fundamental desire to learn about most brands, and they are typically not relationship-oriented when it comes to products and brands. In other words, most consumers are generally apathetic towards most product and brands they buy, do not know much about them, and do not necessarily want to learn about them.

Consider for example evidence that 77% of people, when asked, say they do not have a relationship with any brand. In addition, research shows that 80% of a brand's buyers know little or nothing about the brand, and 50% of all knowledge about a brand is held by just 20% of its buyers. So, most consumers are not that interested in brands, and only a small minority have significant knowledge of a given brand. Consumers' interest in brands seems to peak only in the presence of incentives. For example, data suggests that the number 1 reason why customers interact with brands on social sites is to get a discount. And most customers are also generally not interested in the immersive experiences that brands like to offer online, even if they are designed to entertain.

Moreover, most customers are not fully loyal to any given brand for a long time. Instead, they tend to be polygamously loyal (i.e., they will buy from several different brands over an extended period of time) rather than fully loyal to a given brand. For example, research shows that 72% of Pepsi drinkers also drink Coca-Cola. And most decision making, especially for consumer products, is fast. Breakfast cereal is typically chosen in less than 23 seconds. So, customer inertia, or auto-pilot, is possibly a more important influence on customer behaviour than anything a marketer can do.

The implication of this is that a brand's health depends on lots of people who don't know the brand very well, don't think very much of it, and don't buy it all that often. In order to defeat this fundamental apathy in consumers, brands need to stand out and be distinctive, not just different. While differentiation focuses on meeting personal needs in a different way, distinctiveness is about reducing consumers' cognitive effort. The more consumers can rely on an implicit reaction to a brand, the more likely they are to buy it. So the trick is to create a brand experience that truly resonates and lingers with customers, and to create both physical and mental availability. Physical availability is about making the brand accessible (e.g., ensuring that customers can find it wherever and whenever they would expect to find it). Mental availability is the propensity for a brand to be noticed and/or thought of in buying situations. Building mental availability requires creativity and distinctive, clear branding.

For example, by 2010 Old Spice had become a declining brand with poor sales and a weak image in the marketplace. It had become the aftershave brand someone's grandfather would buy, and it did not resonate with younger consumers. In 2010 the brand hired the advertising agency W+K, which believed the brand was in urgent need of an injection of distinctiveness. The result was a very creative campaign ("the man your man could smell like") that boosted the mental availability of Old Spice among younger buyers, and completely turned the brand around. First, videos were launched on YouTube, to generate buzz among younger consumers by using humour and catching their attention in a completely novel way. Later, TV commercials were also used. Through quirkiness, humour and honesty, these ads created a persona that consumers could relate to, and importantly, remember. They broke through the formulaic ads that were commonplace in the category, stood out and caught people's attention, which ultimately translated into vastly increased sales for the brand.

4.3 PRICING

From the point of view of the customer, whatever is being bought must be perceived to be of greater value than the sum of its costs over the entire ownership of the product. We already mentioned in Part I that price is a combination of tangible and intangible elements that the customer gives up in order to acquire some benefits from a product. Therefore, price is not merely something financial that is incurred once when the product is acquired. There are other components of price as well. Therefore, besides being able to manipulate the monetary element of price, an organisation can also vary other elements.

A useful way to think about price is as the cost of receiving the benefits from a product over the life of its ownership. Therefore, price is the sum of all the following factors:

1. *Money*: The monetary component of price. This includes the actual price tag but also any money spent later to service the product, repair it if things go wrong, etc. Therefore, this includes all financial outlays throughout the life of the product.

2. *Time*: The time it takes the customer to decide on a product, acquire it, learn how to use it, maintain it, etc. A distribution strategy that cuts the lead-time gap (i.e., the difference between the time it takes to procure, make and deliver the product, and the time the customer is prepared to wait) will reduce time, and hence perceived price. Also, a well-known brand may have a higher price tag, but because it speeds up decision making through awareness and recognition, it can reduce overall perceptions of price.

3. *Cognitive Activity*: The mental activity involved in acquiring, using and maintaining the product. Again, this component of price may be reduced by activities such as building brand loyalty, managing reference groups (word of mouth), etc. The less we have to think about something (and thus the easier the decision-making process), the lower the overall perceived price to the customer.

4. *Behavioural effort*: The physical effort needed to search for, acquire and maintain the product. If cognitive activity refers to mental effort, this is to do with physical effort. Effective distribution that is as close as possible to the customer (e.g., online ordering over the Internet, direct distribution, etc), ease of use, extensive instructions, installation, are all factors that may help reduce this component of price.

Therefore, when managing the price element of the marketing mix, a marketer need not only be concerned with the monetary component of price, but he or she also needs to manage the time, cognitive activity and behavioural effort elements very carefully. Managing these factors needs to be part of the marketing tactics. Adopting a more complete view of price can lead to better marketing decisions, more customer value and, of course, higher shareholder value in the long term.

Pricing will depend largely on the level of involvement of the customer in the purchase. You may recall that the level of involvement pertains to how frequently and with what level of risk purchases are made.

For high involvement products (i.e., high-risk products that are infrequently bought), marketers may want to remember that customers use an extensive problem-solving process, which means that a lot of information is required. In these cases, price can act as information (i.e., it can be a decision-making heuristic). Price becomes particularly important when other information cannot be processed properly or is difficult to assess. However, in some cases pricing may not always be a key consideration (e.g., when no alternatives are considered).

In contrast, for low involvement products (i.e., low-risk products that may be frequently bought), the decision-making process takes the shape of a limited problem-solving mechanism. Therefore, little information is required for processing and customers usually have an implicit price range (i.e., a mental price range where, as long as the price of the product falls within that range, the purchase is likely to be made). Price is therefore less important as long as it falls within the implicit price range. If not, then customers will consider it as an attribute in the decision-making process.

Figure 35: Pricing objectives

	Skimming	Penetration	Stability
Description	Price high. Often used for new or unique products.	Price low. Often used to compete with substitutes.	Price at industry level. Avoids price wars.
Typical stage of the PLC	Introduction	Growth	Maturity
Primary goal	Sell to inelastic buyers	Grow market share	Preserve price stability
Secondary goal	Maximise short run profits	Maximise long run profitability	Compete based on other factors

4.3.1. Pricing Objectives

One of the most important considerations when designing a pricing strategy for a product pertains to the pricing objectives. Fundamentally, there are 3 main pricing objectives that may be used by organisations:

- *Skimming objective*: The price level is set above the going market rate. The aim is to sell to price-inelastic customers who may then act as opinion leaders or reference groups. After this group has purchased, price may be lowered to capture the remaining groups of adopters. This approach tends to be very short-term oriented and often assumes that competitors will follow quickly. This holds true, unless, of course, the strategy is to have a premium product (e.g., luxury products).

- *Penetration objective*: The price level is set below the going market rate. This approach is typically used in the growth stage of the PLC. It is often based on economies of scale and is used as a weapon to discourage potential new entrants. That is, it makes the industry less attractive to potential entrants. Market share should grow assuming that demand is elastic and there is still little

132

competitive retaliation. This approach usually aims to maximise long-run profitability by establishing dominant market share.

- *Stability objective*: The price level is set at the going market rate. This is the dominant pricing strategy when competition is intense, and customers are price elastic and may swing from one competitor to the other quickly. Competitive activity is based on product improvement, distribution efforts and promotional programmes. In other words, companies will attempt to take pricing out of the equation, when it comes to customer decision-making.

Figure 35 compares the three main pricing approaches depending on the stage of the PLC in which they are mostly employed, and their primary and secondary objectives.

4.3.2. Pricing tactics

Skimming, penetration and stability pricing approaches are the fundamental ways in which we can think about a pricing strategy. Once a business has decided which approach it wishes to adopt, it then needs to develop a more specific pricing structure or tactic. How exactly are prices going to be set? There are at least 8 pricing tactics:

1. Cost-plus pricing

This involves adding a percentage amount to the per-unit cost of making and distributing the product. This way, a manufacturer can, for example, determine exactly how much profit it makes from each sale. While the tactics make sense, they really only work well in monopolies. We can think of cost-plus pricing as a relic of the production orientation era. It is not very effective in most circumstances because it is not driven by the customers' propensity to pay (i.e., we may end up charging too much or too little).

2. Premium launch pricing

This is essentially a skimming strategy designed to extract high profits from lead users. The price is set high as the product is launched, in order to target the lead users who are price inelastic. Afterwards, prices are dropped to target later adoption groups. The problem with this pricing strategy is that it invites competition (as it makes the industry attractive to potential new entrants, due to the high profits being made).

3. Penetration launch pricing

This is a penetration strategy when the initial price at launch is set lower than supply and demand would dictate. The objective is to gain market share at the expense of margins. It can also help in building barriers to entry. However, of course, it tends to attract bargain hunters who may not necessarily be very profitable customers.

4. Experience curve pricing

This tactic involves progressively lowering the price as the company is able to cover its cost of production. The early entrant can benefit from process improvements over time, which continuously reduces the company's costs. Thus, the company is able to charge lower and lower prices. This can act as a powerful barrier to potential new entrants, who would always be behind the experience curve. It clearly rewards a first mover.

5. Prestige pricing

A business can create a perception of brand quality or exclusivity by setting a high price. In these cases, the behaviour of buyers runs counter to the economic law of demand, which states that demand increases as price decreases. Sometimes, a higher price can actually lead to higher demand for products.

6. Bait and hook pricing

This tactic involves setting the initial price low but charging aggressively for replacement parts or other products consumed during the product's life. This is often used for products such as razor blades, computer printers, etc. A customer may buy a printer for $99 and think it is great value, until he or she needs a new toner cartridge that costs $150! Of course, the risk to companies using this pricing tactic is that makers of generic replacement parts may enter the market attracted by high profits.

7. Promotion pricing

This involves temporarily reducing the price or offer rebates. It can be used to build interest and launch a new product, to steal customers from the competition, to reduce excess inventory, or simply to prevent customer defection. The main risks of this tactic, of course, are that people will start to expect price reductions, and they can also cheapen the brand.

8. Value-based pricing

Value-based pricing has been advocated as the best way to price a company's products. The idea is that customer-perceived value is the ultimate arbiter of pricing. This means that one must understand how the people who make purchase decisions assess value. Each segment will place a different value on the product. Then the price must be set according to each segment's propensity to pay. The idea is therefore that some price discrimination is desirable, and that price needs to be based on customer value. Let us look at an example.

Figure 36: Example of value-based pricing

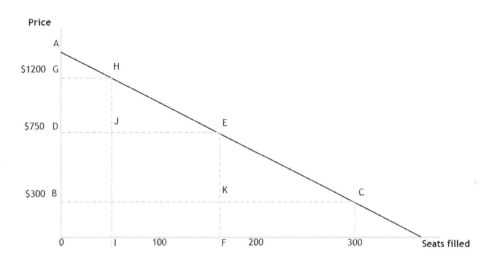

Assume that we are trying to set prices for seats on a London-New York flight in a plane that accommodates up to a total of 300 passengers. The demand curve is depicted in Figure 36 (market research can help develop a curve such as this, by investigating customers' propensity to buy according to different price levels).

At a price of $300, the 300 seats in the plane are filled. The total revenue for this flight is therefore: 300 seats x $300 = $90,000.

However, there is consumer surplus, represented by triangle ABC, which is not captured. Consumer surplus refers to the difference between the

135

amount customers are prepared to pay and how much they actually pay. In fact, many customers who buy the ticket for $300 would have been prepared to pay more for it. Thus, a more profitable price for the ticket would have been $750, which generates more revenue: 160 seats x $750 = $120,000. However, at this price, only 160 seats are filled. Revenue from the remaining seats is lost.

The solution to this pricing problem is to charge different prices to different customers, according to their propensity to pay. For example, the airline may choose the following pricing structure:

First class seats: 50 seats at $1200

Business class seats: 110 seats at $750

Economy class seats: 140 seats at $300

The total revenue from this flight is now a more attractive $184,500.

Even more consumer surplus could be captured (triangles AGH, HJE and EKC), for instance, by price customisation (e.g., the airline could charge economy class passengers different prices depending on when they book, whether the ticket is refundable, whether frequent flyer miles are accrued from the flight, whether they have check-in baggage or not, etc.). Furthermore, the airline also needs to manage the added cost of offering premium class travellers extra benefits that deliver value to them while still profiting from the sale of the seat.

Let us look at another example of a company that implemented value-based pricing after years of setting prices just based on competitive parity. The company is a human resources website that allows employers to post jobs for a fee, which job seekers can then look up and apply for. Customers range from early-stage companies to large established organisations. Since inception, the price was set to $99 a month regardless, for instance, the company size.

The HR company suspected that if they implemented value-based pricing they could improve returns, so they set up a pricing experiment, where each new customer was charged a different price. For a month, every new organisation that came to the site and was a new customer, was assigned to one of 10 different price groups. For example, some of them were quoted a monthly price of $19, others the usual $99, and some $199, $299 or as much as $399. The experiment involved 8000 new customers, and they were all start-ups. The service provided after the clients accepted the price was exactly the same. The company was initially worried that they would lose money by doing this experiment, as they would drive too much business away. Instead, the company made a profit during the experiment: if they had charged everyone $99, the total revenue would have been 13% lower than what they got from the experiment. Because it turns out that while a lot of people obviously paid $19, quite a few also paid $299! The company was surprised that their customers were so price inelastic. That's symptomatic of a company that was charging a price that was not aligned with the value it delivered.

4.4. DISTRIBUTION

Channels are a series of organisations or individuals that connect the producer to the end-user. Distribution refers to the means by which a producer makes its products available to the final customer. Channels are important because they create time, place and possession utilities (i.e., the make products available to customers at the right time, in the right location and in right quantity).

Channels play a number of important functions, which may be grouped into four categories:

- *Informing*: A distribution channel informs customers about the company's products. It can also inform the company about customers' needs.
- *Selling*: The company needs to promote its products and negotiate on prices and terms. The channel facilitates the process.
- *Delivering*: Goods have to be stored and transferred to the customer. Distribution and logistics can be crucial business activities.
- *Financing*: Inventories, accounts receivable and associated risks have to be managed and financed as well.

Fundamentally, there are three main distribution methods available to organisations:

1. *Direct distribution systems*: they refer to company-owned means of distribution. Directly controlled and owned by the company and dedicated only to company products. For example, a sales force. Advantages include more control over distribution, less likelihood of opportunistic behaviour, and closeness to customers.

2. *Indirect systems*: under this system companies do not sell directly to the final user but instead use intermediaries. Intermediaries may be agents, distributors, wholesalers and retailers. Advantages

include lower costs and risks, superior customer reach (because of market coverage customers may already have developed buying patterns), access to experience and customer base.

3. *Mixed or hybrid systems*: these systems involve a combination of direct and indirect systems. This may be because of (1) different channels for different segments, or (2) different channels for the same customers (e.g., the channels carry out complimentary functions).

Figure 37 compares the advantages and disadvantages of direct and indirect approaches to distribution.

Figure 37: Pros and cons of the main distribution methods

	Pros	Cons
Direct	Control	Costly
	Dedicated to the company's products	Risky
		Often limited market coverage
	Close to user	
Indirect	Low cost	Loss of control
	Market reach	Opportunistic behaviour
	Access to experience and information	Conflict

4.4.1. Factors to consider in channel design

The choice of a direct versus an indirect distribution strategy will depend on a number of factors. In general, the following factors should be considered when selecting a distribution strategy:

- *Product characteristics*: For example, the level of product involvement, perishability, whether it requires installations and maintenance, the degree of customisation, product newness, etc.
- *Customer characteristics*: These include the frequency and size of purchase, the amount and type of information required, the problem-solving process, the geographical dispersion of the market, etc.

- *Product life cycle*: Channels should adapt as the product moves from introduction to decline. Over the PLC, channels generally have a decreasing role in adding value to the product.
- *Intermediary characteristics*: For example, do intermediaries know better? Do they have an established customer base the business can tap into?
- *Company characteristics*: The firm's size, its financial resources, the need for control, its product mix etc. should all be considered.
- *Competition*: The level and type of competition will also dictate a channel's structure. Some channels may be used to avoid intense competition or to adopt a niche strategy.

4.4.2. Choices with indirect channels

If a company decides to use an indirect channel, it then needs to make at least two other important strategic decisions: (1) The market coverage strategy (this refers to the number of intermediaries it will use) and (2) whether it will use a conventional or coordinated vertical structure. Let us discuss these choices in some more detail:

1. Market Coverage

Three choices are typically available to companies:

1. *Intensive distribution*: involves selling through all possible wholesalers and retailers that will stock the product. Customers expect to find these products everywhere. Used in particular with convenience goods (e.g., staples, emergency, impulse products).

2. *Exclusive distribution*: selling through only one intermediary in one geographical area. The firm is then able to control prices and the level of service. It is usually based on some agreement that the channel members will buy all or most of a given product from the seller. In return, these are granted exclusive rights. Some intermediaries are so keen to secure the exclusive right to distribution that they will do almost everything to satisfy the producers' demands. It is employed in particular with specialty goods (e.g., cars, watches, etc.).

3. *Selective distribution*: distributing through selected intermediaries only. Only the better intermediaries are used in this case. It allows some advantages from exclusive distribution while still achieving fair market coverage. Used in particular with shopping goods (e.g., clothes, appliances, etc.)

2. Traditional channels or Vertical Marketing Systems (VMSs)?

Traditional marketing channels are often associated with high levels of conflict and opportunistic behaviour. VMSs have developed as an alternative, to ensure cooperation based on the following assumption: if the final consumer does not buy the product, the whole channel suffers. Therefore, it makes sense for the whole channel to act as a unified system.

VMS have emerged as the dominant mode of distribution in consumer marketing. As a result, complete channels now tend to compete against other complete channels. Previously, competition occurred principally between opposing channel members at different levels of the same channel.

There are 3 main types of VMSs:

- *Corporate VMS*: Involves corporate ownership throughout the channel (for example, through acquisitions of other organisations, and in particular, vertical integration). This VMS is distinct from going direct because the organisation is actually carrying out distinct manufacturing, wholesaling and retailing activities.

- *Contractual VMS*: In this VMS, members agree by contract to co-operate with each other. Examples include franchises, such as 7-Eleven and McDonalds.

- *Administered VMS*: This is an informal agreement to cooperate, usually based on the influence of a dominant member of the system. It requires one member of the channel (usually the producer) to be recognised as the leader. For example, a company such as Procter and Gamble employs this system to a large extent.

5 BRANDING

Brands are becoming increasingly important strategic assets of organisations. A brand is not simply a name or a logo. Brands are the set of associations in the minds of customers about the service, product or experience that the organisation delivers. A brand can use a number of elements, such as a name, term, sign, symbol, or design which is intended to identify the goods or services and to differentiate them from those of your competitors. The original motivation for branding was for craftsmen to identify the fruits of their labour, so that customers could easily recognise them. Stamps of trustworthy potters, for example, were relied upon by buyers as a sign of quality. In modern times, tobacco and pharmaceutical products were among the first to be branded. Potions for example, had distinctive labels. Tobacco sellers quickly found out in the 1800s that attractive packages were seen as important.

Nowadays, the new form of competition is less between what companies produce in their factories and more between what they add to their factory output in the form of packaging, services, advertising, customer advice and other things customers value. A brand is more than just a product, because it can have dimensions that differentiate it in some way from other products designed to satisfy the same need. These dimensions may be rational or symbolic. By creating perceived differences among products through branding, and by building a loyal customer base, marketers create value that can translate into financial profits. Some brands create competitive advantages with product performance (e.g., Gillette, Merck), for example, when the brand stands for innovation and leading-edge products. Other brands create competitive advantages through non-product-related means (e.g., Coca-Cola, Chanel), for example, because the brand stands for relevant and appealing images. The main objective of branding is that customers notice the differences among the observed brands in a given product category.

A brand is a perceptual entity: it's something that resides in the minds of consumers. Therefore, pretty much anything can be branded:

- *Physical goods*: Coca-Cola, Mercedes, Nescafe, Sony are all examples of tangible products that have been branded very successfully.

- *Services*: Swiss International Airlines, American Express, Hilton, FedEx are services with strong brands. This is where growth in branding has been felt the most over the last 30 years. Symbols

141

and branding reduce intangibility and make something abstract more concrete. For this reason, branding has become a key competitive weapon in services. British Airways uses the brands "Club class" for business class and "World Traveller" for economy; a clever way to communicate to the regular passengers that they are also special in some way.

- *Retailers*: Retailers like Harrods and Macy's have their own strong brand with unique associations. In retailing, brands can generate loyalty and communicate to customers that they can expect a certain range of products. For example, the UK retailer Tesco communicates large assortment and good prices. Its competitor Waitrose is about higher-end, more selected items. Retailers can also launch their own store brands or private labels as another way to generate revenue.

- *Online companies*: Dot.coms such as Google and Amazon had to build their brand from scratch, in order to create a position in the mind of consumers, and to foster recognition and interest. Traditional bricks and mortar firms can use the internet to leverage their existing brand.

- *People and organisations*: Politicians, sports people, entertainers, and organisations like the National Geographic have also discovered the power of branding. The American actor Paul Newman leveraged his likeable image to launch Newman's Own, a brand of sauces, after friends and family encouraged him to do so after trying his home-made salad dressings and pasta sauces. The brand has been very successful and donates all profits to charity. But of course, one does not have to be a celebrity to see oneself as a brand. For example, in the job market we all have to strengthen our own brand!

- *Sports, arts etc*: Real Madrid, Harry Potter and the Beatles are all very strong brands. For example, every sequel of the Harry Potter story is a brand extension that relies on the show's initial popularity. When we watch a sequel, we know what to expect. This is a classic application of branding.

- *Geographic locations*: Places such as a country or a city can be branded very effectively. This could be done to entice temporary visits, permanent moves or business investment.

- *Ideas and causes*: Even ideas and causes can be branded effectively, and unique associations be leveraged to create awareness and interest among people. This can be especially important for non-profit organisations, such as WWF or Greenpeace. The latter had used very sophisticated marketing and branding messages over the years to get their points across.

5.1 Why do Brands Matter?

Brands are important because they can create value for both the organisation that owns them and its customers.

Brands play many important roles for customers. These include:

- Identification of source of product
- Assignment of responsibility to product maker
- Promise from the producer, a bond or pact with the producer
- Signal of quality
- Symbolic device
- Purchase risk reducer
- Search cost reducer

Through experience, customers find out which brands satisfy their needs and which ones do not. Based on what they already know about the brand (e.g., its quality, characteristics, etc.) consumers can make assumptions and form reasonable expectations about what they may not know about the brand. For this reason, well known brands can speed up decision making and reduce search cost. Importantly, brands can also reduce purchase risk, such as financial risk (e.g., the cost involved in dealing with problems if the brand does not perform as expected), time risk (e.g., the time taken to make decision and address potential problems), social risk (e.g., the perceptions that other people may have of us using a specific brand), physical risk (e.g., any potential personal hazard), and functional risk (e.g., will the product perform as promised?). Consider, for example, a brand like iPhone, and how it reduces purchase risk for its buyers (e.g., some consumers may buy the new model because they know it will work, they may want to project an image of themselves, etc.).

Of course, strong brands are also crucial to those organisations that own them and manage them effectively. The valuable functions provided by brands to their firms include the following:

- Brands as signals of identification with the aim to make tracing and handling simpler
- Means of legally protecting unique features

- Signal of quality level
- Bestow products with unique associations
- Provide competitive advantage and enhance financial returns

In some cases, the contribution of the brand to the financial value generated by a firm can be very high, possibly even higher than any other asset. A company like Coca-Cola, for example, has a brand that has been estimated to be worth about $75 billion. It is interesting to look at that brand value as a percentage of Coca-Cola's market capitalization. Market capitalization is a measurement of corporate size equal to the share price multiplied by the number of shares outstanding. As a measure, it can represent the public opinion of a company's net worth and is a determining factor in stock valuation. Coca-Cola's market capitalization is approximately $170 billion at the time of writing. This means that about 45% of the value generated in the market by Coca-Cola is due solely to its brand!

5.2 BRAND EQUITY

Brand equity is defined as the differential effect the knowledge of the brand has on how consumers respond to a brand's marketing. Building and managing brand equity over time is a key strategic imperative for many firms. The power of brands lies in what customers have learned, felt, seen, and heard about the brand as a result of their experiences over time. In other words, the power of a brand lies in what resides in the minds of customers (i.e., brand equity).

A brand has positive brand equity when consumers react more favourably to a product and its marketing mix when the brand is identified than when it is not. On the other hand, a brand has negative equity when customers react less favourably to marketing activities for the brand compared to an unnamed or fictitious version of the product.

Marketers face the challenge of ensuring that their consumers form unique and desirable associations, feelings, beliefs, images and perceptions about their brands through positive experiences with the product or service. So, there are 3 key ingredients of customer-based brand equity:

- *A differential effect*: the brand must create some difference in the minds of customers, and consequently may get customers to behave differently.

- *Brand knowledge*: these differences are a result of customers' knowledge of what the brand is and what it stands for (i.e., it resides in the mind of customers).

- *Consumer response to marketing*: all the elements of the marketing mix (particularly advertising) will build and reinforce what is in the mind of customers.

At the simplest level, brand equity is generated when the company manages two equally important sides of the same coin, as pictured in Figure 38 below.

Figure 38: The Two Key Elements of Brand Equity

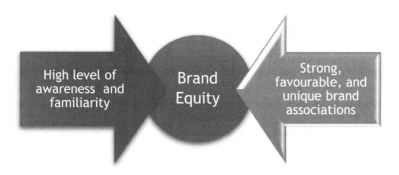

The figure above shows that customer-based brand equity occurs when:

1. *The consumer has a high level of awareness of the brand.*

   Brand awareness has a number of key benefits. (1) *Learning benefits*: it makes it easy for customers to learn about the brand. Once the brand is in memory, customers can begin to build brand associations. (2) *Evoked set benefits*: awareness increases the likelihood that the brand will be part of the evoked set (i.e., a mental list of brands that are considered for purchase in a certain product category). (3) *Choice advantage*: Higher awareness of a brand may lead to choosing that brand over others, even though there are no other associations to that brand. This is particularly true for low involvement purchases, where product choices are based purely on recognition.

2. *The consumer holds some strong, favourable, and unique brand association in memory (i.e., brand image).*

> To create a positive brand image, you need to link strong, favourable and unique associations to the brand. "Strong" means that the marketing manager has to make the brand messages consistent, and the brand relevant to customers. "Favourable" means that you need to position the brand in a way that is desired by customers (i.e., make it positive). Moreover, "unique" means that you need to build a sustainable competitive advantage by giving customers something different.

> Of course, customers can form these associations in a variety of ways. For example, they can originate through personal experiences with the brand, through promotion such as advertising, through consumer reports, word of mouth of other customers, by assumption based on the brand name, logo, etc. So, the marketing mix is not the only direct way in which we can build a brand image. The wise marketer will leverage all vehicles. For example, Google does very little advertising, but yet it has a very unique and strong brand image.

> Sources of associations can also include product-related elements (e.g., the benefits of the product, features, characteristics, etc.) and non-product related elements: (e.g., emotional connections, etc.).

Each of the two components of brand equity is a necessary but not sufficient element of brand equity. In other words, both are typically required in order to build brand equity. There are some exceptions to this rule: in some cases, for very low-involvement and perhaps unimportant purchases, awareness alone can be enough to trigger consumer's decision.

5.2.1. Branding and storytelling

Building brand associations in the mind of customers essentially involves crafting a story around the brand and telling that story as effectively as possible to customers. As Steve Jobs famously said, "th*e most powerful person in the world is the storyteller*". Indeed, it is no coincidence that Apple has become such a successful brand globally, by constantly and consistently telling a story that is about innovation, thinking differently and challenging conventions.

Similarly, Seth Godin, the influential American writer and marketer, once pointed out: "marketing is no longer about the stuff that you make, but about the stories you tell." This suggests that brands need to make an emotional impact on consumers if they want to win them over and sharing a compelling story can help them do that.

In general, the most effective stories are those that are forged best by identifying solidly with specific archetypes. Archetypes are patterns we are all familiar with, or mental images present in the collective unconscious. They are symbols of meaning that our minds easily recognise. Different kinds of stories—such as in a novel or a movie for example—regularly employ archetypes to make storytelling more efficient and effective. For example, Shakespeare relied on several archetypes in his storytelling, such as the fool (who we expect to be silly and funny), the hero (who is usually set up to be the protagonist with which we may identify with) and the princess in distress (who we expect to be saved by the hero).

An archetype is like a code that we use to understand things. It guides us in terms of what to expect, and for that reason, it can simplify storytelling. Instead of having to reinvent a character from scratch every time, evoking specific archetypes acts as a shortcut that immediately creates a set of expectations and associations in the minds of our audience. Archetypes can be useful to communicate effectively, make a psychological connection with our audience, and build an emotional attachment.

Marketers can attach archetypes to a brand in order to make a psychological connection with the consumer. The archetypes can act as heuristics, or shortcuts for the consumer to build an emotional attachment with the brand. For example, Nike has regularly and consistently evoked the archetype of the hero in its brand-related storytelling. Archetypes can be very useful in branding, by representing the brand's role and purpose in a form that everyone recognises immediately.

Marketers have to be clear about what archetype they are evoking for their brand in order to avoid mixed messages. Consciously or unconsciously, consumers want to know what a brand stands for and they value consistency. If a brand consistently evokes a particular archetype, customers will feel they know who it is and can trust it to behave in a certain way. In a way, they will feel safer around the brand. While consumers can identify with a variety of archetypes, strong brands are forged best by identifying solidly with just one archetype (or maybe two, but usually not more) that helps to create a focus around the brand. If a brand identifies with too many archetypes, its story becomes diluted and ineffective.

Margaret Mark and Carol Pearson in their book "The Hero and the Outlaw" establish the case for twelve brand archetypes based upon a quadrant of opposing psychological needs: stability *vs* risk, and independence *vs* belonging. Their framework is depicted in Figures 39 and 40.

Figure 39. Brand archetypes: purpose, associations and examples

Archetype	Purpose	Main associations and cues	Examples
Innocent	Safety Seeks purity, goodness and happiness	Purity, goodness, happiness, simple, trust, honesty, rebirth, perfectionist, naïve, mystic	Dove, Qantas, Sesame Street
Sage	Understanding Helps people understand their world	Knowledge, wisdom, expert, truth, think, understand, interpret, progress, mentor, teach	Audi, Discovery Channel, TED
Explorer	Freedom Explores and discovers	Discover, seek, wander, find out, adventure, individual, pioneer, freedom, risk, fearless, curious, experience	The North Face, National Geographic, GoPro
Outlaw	Liberation Rebels and breaks the rules	Rule breaker, rebel, revolutionary, disrupt, destroy, outrageous, radical, unconventional, outsider	Virgin, Harley Davidson, MTV
Magician	Power Transforms situations	Vision, transform, change, win-win, charisma, miracles, makes dreams come true	Disney, Tesla, Mastercard
Hero	Mastery Acts courageously to put things right	Courage, challenge, competition, strong, powerful, determination, prevail, persevere, warrior, turnaround	Nike, BMW, Duracell
Lover	Intimacy Finds and gives love and sensual pleasure	Partner, intimate, harmony, pleasure, intimacy, beautiful, relationship, attractive, passion, gratitude, friendship	Chanel, Ferrari, Victoria's Secret
Jester	Enjoyment Has a god time but conveys serious message	Live for the moment, impulsive, entertain, playful, clever, outrageous, light-hearted, fun.	Skittles, Fanta, Ben & Jerry's

Every-man	Belonging Ok as they are, connect with others	Connect, belong, friend, down to earth, functional, wholesome, realist, team spirit, unpretentious	IKEA, eBay, The Gap
Care-giver	Service Helps and protects from harm	Care, help, protect, comfort, nurture, parent, support, affection, empathy, commitment, friendly, concern.	Heinz, Johnson & Johnson, Amnesty International
Ruler	Control Takes control, creates order	Control, order, authority, power, substance, impressive, organiser, responsible, boss	Rolex, Mercedes, IBM
Creator	Innovation. Compelled to create an innovate	Create, innovate, vision, invent, inspire, dream, fantasy, experiment, unconventional, beauty, aesthetic	Apple, Swatch, Lego

Figure 40: Brand archetypes

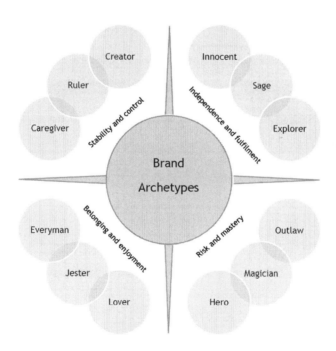

These brand archetypes can help brands connect with their customers in an effective and focused way. Once selected, the archetype of a brand defines the brand's personality and how it presents itself to the world. It determines the entire brand experience at every touchpoint, from the language and imagery used in advertising, to packaging, web design, and so on. Consider, for example, how every detail about Apple—from its product aesthetics to its customer service ethos, from the image of its founder Steve Jobs to its retail store design, and from its packaging to its advertising campaigns—is carefully crafted in such a way to convey the archetype of the creator, who challenges convention to inspire its customers to "Think Different". This is how strong brands tell their story.

5.3 The Brand Management Process

We have argued that strategic brand management involves the design and implementation of marketing programmes and activities to build, measure, and manage brand equity. Thus, the brand management process may be summarised in four steps, which are outlined below in Figure 41.

Figure 41. Steps of the brand management process

5.3.1. Establish brand positioning and values

The first step of the brand management process involves establishing what the brand represents and how it should be positioned. This is about creating competitive superiority in the minds of customers by building points of difference while at the same time establishing points of parity to alleviate concerns about any possible weaknesses. Thus, the concept of positioning covered earlier in section 3.4.2. becomes particularly important for a brand.

Keller's brand equity pyramid model (depicted in Figure 42) is a useful framework to understand how brand equity is built. The model argues that to in order to establish brand positioning and values that drive brand equity, marketers should follow a sequence of 4 steps. Each of these steps is contingent on achieving the objectives of the previous one. The four steps are:

1. Make sure customers identify with the brand and have specific associations in their minds that link the brand to a product class or their needs.

2. Ensure that the brand meaning is strongly established in consumer's minds by creating and strategically linking the brand with tangible and intangible associations.

3. Brand identification and brand meaning should trigger desirable customer responses.

4. The positive brand response should then trigger an intense, active sense of loyalty and establish a loyal relationship between the brand and the consumer.

Figure 42. The brand equity pyramid

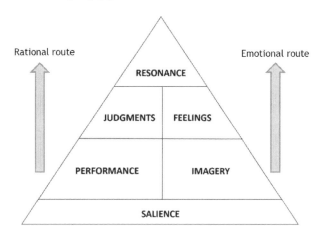

Ultimately, these four steps represent a set of key questions that customers ask about a brand:

1. Who are you? → Brand identity

2. What are you? → Brand meaning

3. What about you? What do I, as a customer, think or feel about you, as a brand? → Brand responses

4. What about you and me? What are the associations I have about you, and do I have a connection with you? → Brand relationship

The framework argues that we cannot establish meaning unless we have created identity; responses cannot happen unless we have developed the right meaning; and we cannot forge a relationship unless we have elicited the proper responses. Once we have established all the brand building blocks with customers, significant brand equity may result.

The blocks on the left represent a more rational route to brand building. In contrast, blocks on the right represent a more emotional route. While strong brands are generally built by going up both sides of the pyramid, in general some brands tend to rely more on emotional elements to build brand equity (e.g., Dior and Chanel), while others take a more rational route (e.g., Roche and ABB).

1. *Salience*: Salience captures the level of awareness of the brand. For instance, how often and how easily the brand is evoked in a particular circumstance. To what extent is the brand top-of-mind and easily recognised and recalled? A salient brand has both depth and breadth of awareness:
    a) Depth: how likely is it that the brand comes to mind? A brand we easily recall has a deeper level of brand awareness.
    b) Breadth: the range of purchase and usage situations in which the brand element comes to mind.

Therefore, the brand doesn't only have to be at the top of the mind (depth), it also has to do so at the right time and in the right places (breadth).

2. *Meaning*: Meaning refers to the different types of associations related to either performance or imagery that may become linked to the brand. Brand meaning is what helps to produce brand responses, or what customers think and feel about the brand.
    a) Performance: The product or service, in the end, is at the heart of brand equity, hence customer expectations have to be met. Brand performance describes how well the product meets customers' functional needs and quality. Brand performance goes beyond the product features, and also includes dimensions that differentiate the brand. These include both primary characteristics and supplementary features, such as product reliability, durability, serviceability, service effectiveness, style, design and price.
    b) Imagery: Brand imagery is about how customers think about a brand abstractly, rather than what they think the

152

brand actually does. These include the intangible aspects of the brand. They may develop through experience, word of mouth, advertising, etc. There are many intangibles, such as user profiles (the type of person who uses the brand), purchase and usage situations (under what conditions they can or should buy the brand), personality (e.g., they may be seen as 'old fashioned', 'modern', 'exotic', etc.), values (such as sincerity, excitement, competence, sophistication and ruggedness) and history and heritage.

3. *Responses*: Brand meaning helps produce brand responses and helps explore what customers think and feel about the brand. We can distinguish brand responses as either brand judgments or brand feelings, that is, in terms of whether they arise from the "head" or from the "heart":
   a) Brand judgments: customers' personal opinions about and evaluations of the brand, which consumers form by putting together all the different brand performance and imagery associations. Customers may make all types of judgments with respect to a brand, for example about its quality, credibility, superiority, and whether it is considered for future purchase.
   b) Brand feelings: customers' emotional responses and reactions to the brand. Does the marketing programme of the brand evoke any feelings in customers, and if so, what kind of feelings? How does the brand affect customers' feelings? These feelings can be mild or intense, and positive or negative. There are several important types of brand-building feelings, such as warmth, fun, excitement, safety, social approval, and self-respect.

4. *Resonance*: the extent to which customers feel they are "in sync" with the brand. Brands which highly resonate with customers include Harley-Davidson, Apple or eBay. Resonance has the following key building blocks:
   a) Behavioural loyalty
   b) Frequency and amount of repeat purchases - How often do customers purchase the brand and how much of it?
   c) Attitudinal attachment – behavioural loyalty is important but not sufficient for resonance to occur. Some customers may buy

simply out of necessity or because they have no choice. Resonance also requires a strong personal attachment: customers may admire the brand or be proud of it.

d) Sense of community – social community is defined as a social phenomenon in which the customer feels part of a community associated with the brand. For example, Apple forums and user groups have become popular. A strong sense of community among loyal users can engender favourable brand attitudes.

e) Active engagement – perhaps the strongest affirmation of brand loyalty occurs when customers are engaged with, or willing to invest time, energy and money in the brand beyond those expended when buying or using the brand. For instance, they may join a club, exchange opinions, participate in chat rooms, etc. In some cases, these customers may become the evangelists of the brand.

Thus, brand resonance, and the relationships customers have with brands, has two dimensions: intensity (i.e., the strength of the attitudinal attachment and sense of community) and activity (i.e., how frequently the buyer buys and uses the brand, as well as engages in other activities not related to just purchase and consumption).

In summary, each step of the brand pyramid model highlights some general objectives to build brand equity:

1. Identity (salience): Develop deep and broad brand awareness

2. Meaning (performance and imagery): Focus on points of parity and points of difference

3. Response (judgments and feelings): Develop positive, accessible reactions

4. Relationships (resonance): Ensure that you build intense, active loyalty

5.3.2. Design the brand marketing programme

Building brand equity requires creating a brand that consumers are sufficiently aware of and with which they have strong, favourable, and unique brand associations. There are 3 factors needed to build brand equity:

1. *Choosing brand elements*: This involves selecting all those devices that serve to identify and differentiate the brand, such as brand names, logos, slogans, etc. The brand elements selected should have specific objectives: increase brand awareness, help in forming unique, strong and favourable associations and induce positive brand feelings and judgements. For maximum effectiveness, brand elements should have the following characteristics: memorability (they build brand awareness through ease of recognition and recall), meaningfulness (e.g., it communicates the positioning), likability (whether customers find the brand element interesting or aesthetically appealing), transferability (e.g., across languages but also within and across product categories, such as the Amazon.com brand, which from the very start lent itself well to the sale of a wide variety of goods, not just books), adaptability (most brand elements have to be adapted over time, because they need to remain contemporary and adapt to changing needs, hence flexibility can prove useful), and protectability (e.g., it can me trademarked). The usual brand elements include:

   a) *Brand names*: captures the key associations and the focal theme of the product in a succinct, economic way.

   b) *URLs*: Universal Resource Locators, or domain names. The number of these increases every day and finding and registering a unique one has become more difficult. Generic URLs, like business.com or internet.com were sold and bought for millions but have now become a liability, as customers prefer more specific, rather than generic, web names.

   c) *Logos and symbols*: All visual elements are important, not just the brand name. Brand like Coca-Cola and Kit Kat have successfully used words as their logos. Others, like Mercedes, Nike and Rolex, have used abstract logos (symbols).

   d) *Characters*: these take on human or real-life characteristics. They are usually introduced through advertising. Can enhance likeability and awareness.

   e) *Slogans*: Short phrases that communicate descriptive or persuasive information about the brand. Most often used in advertisings, they can also appear on packaging. Very helpful to expand on the brand name, communicate the positioning, and highlight the PODs. Examples include Gillette's: The Best a Man Can Get, or Avis': We Try Harder.

f) *Jingles*: musical messages written around the brand. They are similar to extended musical slogans. They can help to increase memorability (e.g., customers will remember it for a while after seeing an ad).

g) *Packaging*: activities of designing and producing containers or wrappers for a product. They help identify the brand, convey information, facilitate storage and transport, and in some cases aid product consumption. Aesthetic considerations are crucial and can allow a product to stand out and communicate the appropriate message. Examples include the shape of Coca-Cola bottles or the green Heineken bottles.

When choosing the brand elements, marketers may like to keep them short and easy to pronounce to enhance memorability; and to create differentiation, they may want to make them distinctive.

2. *Integrating the brand into marketing activities*: while brand elements are important, the whole marketing mix makes a significant contribution towards creating strong, favourable and unique associations. Advertising, in particular, whether online or offline is a key element of a branding programme. It is important though to remember that consumers are not naturally a captive audience. In other words, they are not as interested in brands as marketers often seem to assume. Research has shown that most customers do not say they have a relationship with brands, and they do not really engage with brands on social media. Most of the knowledge about a brand is held by a small portion of its buyers, and most of a brand's buyers know little or nothing about that brand. Generally, customers do not enjoy learning about brands and like to make decisions quickly. Therefore, a brand's health depends on lots of people who don't know it very well, don't think very much of it, and don't buy it that often. As a consequence, brands need to stand out in an increasingly cluttered world where customers are mostly apathetic. This requires building brand distinctiveness, not just brand differentiation. Any part of the brand experience can help a brand craft a story around who they are, making sure the story resonates and lingers with customers. Colours, logos, taglines, symbols, endorsements, highly creative advertisements

can all help. Differentiation focuses on meeting personal needs in a different way, whereas distinctiveness is about reducing consumers' cognitive effort – making buying a brand easier and quicker. The more consumers can rely on an implicit reaction to a brand, the more likely they are to buy that brand. So, strong brands have both physical and mental availability: you should be able to find them in the right place at the right time, and they should have strong salience, i.e., high probability that a consumer would notice, recognise, and think of the brand in a buying situation.

3. *Leveraging secondary associations*: brands may be linked to other brands that have their own associations, and when they do so, they borrow and transfer some of those associations (see Figure 43). When a brand uses a celebrity endorser for example, it tries to transfer some of the association's consumers make with that celebrity to the brand itself. So, when Rolex used Roger Federer in its advertising, it associated itself with world-class performance, success, achievement, etc. Suddenly, whatever people think of Federer is transferred to the Rolex brand. But it's not just about celebrities; other sources of associations include countries (e.g., "made in Italy"), other brands (e.g., Audi offering cars with Bang & Olufsen hi-fi systems), characters (e.g., Disney characters of Kellogg's cereals), channels (e.g., "you can find our brand at Harrod's"), etc. In these cases, the marketer is borrowing associations from other entities. Therefore, brands may be linked to other entities that have their own knowledge structures in consumers' minds. Because of these linkages, consumers may assume that the same associations of the secondary entity apply to the brand Thus, the brand can borrow some brand knowledge and equity from the other entity. There are different means through which we can create secondary brand knowledge by linking the brand to a variety of entities. This strategy is particularly useful for low involvement products or when products are low in search criteria. It works when three factors are in place: awareness and knowledge of the original entity, meaningfulness of the knowledge of the entity, and transferability of the knowledge of the entity.

Figure 43. Potential sources of secondary brand associations

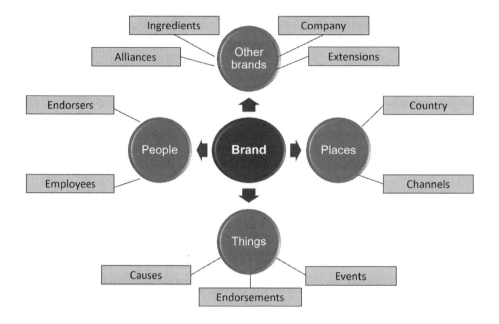

5.3.3. Measure and interpret brand performance

It's important for organisations to measure the performance of their brands. This is because measuring brand equity gives marketing activities board room legitimacy (i.e., it can help shift away from perception of marketing as a cost centre and it elevates marketing expenditure to a strategic level). It can also help coordinate the organisational effort around the brand (i.e., it can mobilise cross-functional support and cooperation, provide an organisation-wide understanding of the activities that build or destroy brand value, and rewards a long-term view in marketing initiatives).

To examine a brand, assess its health, uncover its sources of equity, and suggest ways to improve and leverage that equity, we need to understand the sources of brand equity from both the businesses' and the customer's perspective. The brand value chain (see Figure 44) allows marketers to trace the value creation processes for brands, to better understand the financial impact of branding investments. In order to observe accurate, timely and actionable information about the brand, brand tracking and brand equity management systems can be in place. These tools allow

158

managers to make the best short-term tactical decision, as well as the best long-turn strategic decisions.

Everything begins with the marketing programme investment. However, the ability of a branding investment to affect customer mindset depends on qualitative aspects of the marketing programme, namely its clarity, relevance distinctiveness and consistency. Four dimensions have emerged as particularly important measures of the extent to which the marketing programme has shaped the customer mindset: awareness (brand recall and recognition), associations (strong, unique and favourable), attitudes (such as quality and satisfaction), attachment (e.g., loyalty) and activity (how often do customers use the brand, talk to others, interact around it, etc.). However, even if the customer mindset is shaped in a positive way, the ability to create market performance is still affected by factors beyond the individual customer. For example, competitors may get in the way, with their own marketing efforts, channel support may be lacking, or the customer segment is not large enough to be profitable. Assuming all these factors are positive, a brand can improve market performance: the customer mindset affects how customers behave in the marketplace in many ways, e.g., through price premiums, market share, sales, the possibility of brand expansion, etc. Finally, the ability of the brand value created to reach the final stage in terms of shareholder value creation varies depending on investor sentiment. This may be affected by market dynamics (e.g., interest rates, supply of capital, etc.), growth potential (of the brand and industry), risk profile (how vulnerable is the brand to fluctuations in any factors?) and brand contribution (how important is the brand to the firm's portfolio?). The financial markets eventually formulate an opinion that have very direct financial implications for the brand value. Research has shown that strong brands deliver greater returns to stockholders.

The Brand Value Chain

To examine a brand, assess its health, uncover its sources of equity, and suggest ways to improve and leverage that equity, we need to understand the sources of brand equity from both the businesses' and the customer's perspective. The brand value chain (see Figure 44) allows marketers to trace the value creation processes for brands, to better understand the financial impact of branding investments. In order to observe accurate, timely and actionable information about the brand, brand tracking and brand equity management systems can be in place. These tools allow

159

managers to make the best short-term tactical decision, as well as the best long-turn strategic decisions.

Figure 44. The Brand Value Chain

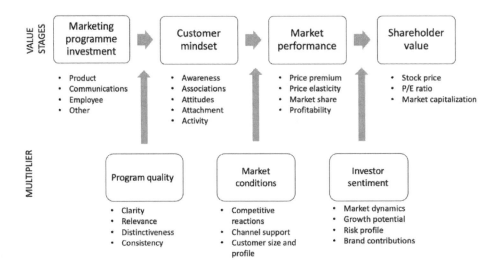

Everything begins with the marketing programme investment. However, the ability of a branding investment to affect customer mindset depends on qualitative aspects of the marketing programme, namely its clarity, relevance distinctiveness and consistency. Four dimensions have emerged as particularly important measures of the extent to which the marketing programme has shaped the customer mindset: awareness (brand recall and recognition), associations (strong, unique and favourable), attitudes (such as quality and satisfaction), attachment (e.g., loyalty) and activity (how often do customers use the brand, talk to others, interact around it, etc.). However, even if the customer mindset is shaped in a positive way, the ability to create market performance is still affected by factors beyond the individual customer. For example, competitors may get in the way, with their own marketing efforts, channel support may be lacking, or the customer segment is not large enough to be profitable. Assuming all these factors are positive, a brand can improve market performance: the customer mindset affects how customers behave in the marketplace in many ways, e.g., through price premiums, market share, sales, the possibility of brand expansion, etc. Finally, the ability of the brand value created to reach the final stage in terms of shareholder value creation

160

varies depending on investor sentiment. This may be affected by market dynamics (e.g., interest rates, supply of capital, etc.), growth potential (of the brand and industry), risk profile (how vulnerable is the brand to fluctuations in any factors?) and brand contribution (how important is the brand to the firm's portfolio?). The financial markets eventually formulate an opinion that have very direct financial implications for the brand value. Research has shown that strong brands deliver greater returns to stockholders.

This Brand Value Chain model has significant implications for marketers. It shows that value creation begins with the marketing programme investment, in the form of a well-funded, well-designed and well-implemented campaign. However, it also requires more than the initial marketing investment: each of the 3 multipliers can increase or decrease market value as it moves from stage to stage, and many of these are outside marketers' control (so, we need to understand them first, before blaming marketers for an unsuccessful campaign!). Importantly, the brand value chain provides us with a detailed road map: there are metrics associated with each stage, which highlight what information is required to understand how brand equity is generated.

The Brand Asset Valuator

The Brand Asset Valuator (BAV) is a useful tool to assess the performance of a brand and derives useful implications for its management. Developed by Young & Rubicam, the BAV is the world's largest database of consumer-derived information on brands. Since 1993, it has used more than 500,000 consumers in more than 40 countries, testing their views on more than 20,000 brands. BAV outcomes have also been linked to financial metrics. In several countries, BAV data is collected quarterly, which allows short-term trends in branding to be analysed.

The BAV is a conceptual model that helps us understand how brands grow and decline and how they drive financial success. It is also a diagnostic tool for measuring brand health, a strategic tool for developing brand vision, and an accountability tool for tracking changes in key brand measures over time. Anyone can use the principles of the BAV without the need for extensive data collection and analysis.

The BAV measures brands on four fundamental measures of equity value and using a set of perceptual dimensions. This measurement allows us to plot brands on a two-by-two matrix as depicted in Figure 45. The BAV argues that brand equity derives from two categories of dimensions:

Figure 45. The Brand Asset Valuator (BAV)

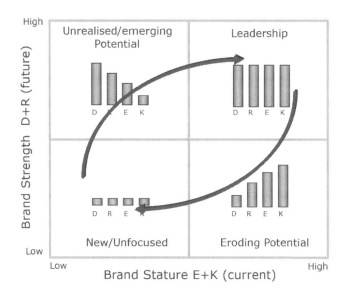

Brand strengths dimensions, which tend to reflect the brand's future value:

1. Differentiation: The degree to which the brand is seen as different from others or has a distinctive meaning.

2. Relevance: It measures the breadth of a brand's appeal and its energy, and how well it fits into people's lives and is in sync with their needs.

Brand stature dimensions, which mostly reflect past performance:

1. Esteem: how well the brand is regarded and respected, how well it is liked.

2. Knowledge: how familiar and intimate consumers are with the brand.

The above four measures are the basis of the below two equations:

Differentiation x Relevance = Brand Strength

Esteem x Familiarity = Brand Stature

162

The magnitude of these factors determines the location of the brand in the strength-stature matrix. Usually successful brands will follow a lifecycle, whereby they will start in the bottom left quadrant and reach leadership by moving first into the upper left quadrant. This is an ideal way to build brand equity, as once strength is in place, stature can follow more easily (the opposite, i.e., a brand trying to build stature first and strength second, is often risky and inefficient). The problem is that once leadership is achieved, brands will naturally tend to fall into the lower right quadrant (and then back to the bottom left), mainly when they fail to sustain their brand strength by protecting their sources of differentiation and relevance.

Depending on the location in the matrix, some basic strategic implications may be derived:

a) Brands generally begin the life in the unfocused quadrant, where they first need to develop relevant differentiation and establish their reason for being.

b) The next step usually leads to emerging potential, as increased differentiation, followed by relevance, initiates a growth in brand strength. These developments take place before the brand has acquired esteem or is widely known. Some niche, specialty brands tend to remain in this quadrant (from the viewpoint of the mass market) and can use their brand strength to occupy a profitable niche.

c) The leadership quadrant is populated by brand leaders, which could be new or established brands. This suggests that brand leadership is truly a function of the pillar measures rather than just longevity.

d) Brands whose strength has declined (often because of falling differentiation) end up in eroding potential. These brands become vulnerable to existing competitors but also private labels and other discount brands. Thus, they may end up stuck in a price war and eventually end up with a declining brand stature.

Figure 46. Hypothetical example of the BAV in the car industry (2020)

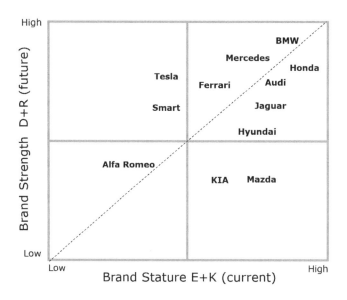

Depending on their position within the BAV, brands will tend to display different profiles in terms of profit margins and growth (see figure 46). It is usually desirable for a brand to be above the diagonal, in a situation where strength is higher than stature (i.e., where the future potential of the brand is higher than its past or current potential). This also means that some brands prefer to remain in the emerging potential quadrant indefinitely (as is the case for highly specialty and exclusive brands).

Marketers can use to BAV to derive some useful implications from the performance of their brands. They can adjust the marketing mix in several ways in order to optimise the brand's position. For example:

a) *New/Unfocused brands*: invest in all factors, and primarily in making the brand strong and unique. If you do that well, awareness and favourability should follow.

b) *Emerging potential brands*: These are often strong new brands. Emphasise the promotional mix to increase awareness and the product mix to increase favourability. Decide whether to increase mass appeal to move into leadership position or maintain a strong position within this quadrant (for example through a niche or luxury strategy).

164

c) *Leadership brands*: manage well the entire marketing mix to maintain this position. Both young and old brands may be found here so time is less important than management of the brand. The tendency for these brands is to fall into eroding potential, so protecting brand strength is paramount.

d) *Eroding potential brands*: These are declining brands. Avoid price-wars due to lack of differentiation and invest into the brand to make it unique again if possible. Some of these brands can return into the leadership quadrant if the brand is re-energised and revitalised.

Figure 47. The Brand Asset Valuator: Profit margin and growth

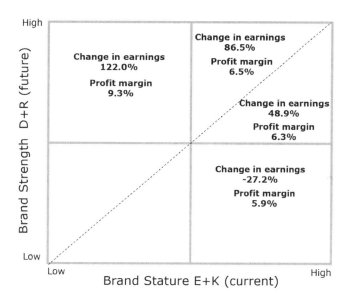

The Interbrand approach

Interbrand's brand valuation methodology places a financial valuation on brands, provides insights into how brands contribute to business performance, and suggests a road map of activities to build brand equity. Interbrand started valuating brands back in the 1980s, based on the premise that strong brands influence customer choice and create loyalty, they attract, retain and motivate talent, and lower the cost of financing. Their brand valuation methodology has been designed to take all of these factors into account and every year they publish a list of the world's most valuable brands on their website.

The Interbrand approach is useful, particularly because it is a step closer to putting a financial value on the brand, and it involves three steps:

1. *Financial Analysis*: The analysis includes the assessment of the financial returns to the investors of the organisation, or the economic profit. Economic profit is the after-tax operating profit of the brand, minus a charge for the capital used to generate the brand's revenue and margins.

2. *Role of Brand*: This measures the portion of the purchase decision attributable to the brand as opposed to other factors (for example, purchase drivers such as price, convenience, or product features). The Role of Brand Index (RBI) quantifies this as a percentage. The Best Global Brands' RBI score is derived through consulting three methods: expert panel assessment, commissioned market research and benchmarks against the RBI scores of industry competitors.

3. *Brand Strength*: Brand Strength is the assessment of the ability of a brand to generate a loyal customer base, hence build sustainable demand for its products, and consequently generate profit. Brand Strength analysis is based on an evaluation across 10 factors that Interbrand believes constitute a strong brand (and which in many ways can be used even on their own as helpful brand management KPIs). Performance is benchmarked against industry competitors and leading brands. The Brand Strength analysis constitutes an assessment of the brand's strengths and weaknesses and can be used to develop a future plan to grow the brand's strength and value. The 10 factors are listed below (the first 4 are internal and the rest are external):

   a) *Clarity*: Being clear about the values, positioning and propositions of the brand, as well as about who the target is, the insights and drivers of customer needs. Because much hinges on this, it is vital that these are articulated internally and shared across the organisation.

   b) *Commitment*: Internal commitment to brand, and a belief internally in the importance of the brand. Commitment also looks at the extent to which the brand receives time, influence and investment.

c) *Protection*: How secure the brand is across a number of dimensions: legal protection, propriety ingredients or design, scale or geographical spread.

d) *Responsiveness*: The ability to respond to market changes, challenges and opportunities. The brand should possess an internal sense of leadership and a desire to evolve and renew in the future.

e) *Authenticity*: The brand is soundly based on an internal truth and capability. The brand should have a well-defined heritage and a grounded value set. The brand should be able to meet customer expectations.

f) *Relevance*: The fit with customer/consumer needs, desires, and decision criteria across all relevant demographics and geographies.

g) *Differentiation*: The extent to which customers/consumers perceive the brand to have a differentiated positioning distinctive from the competition.

h) *Consistency*: The degree to which a brand is experienced without fail across all touchpoints or formats.

i) *Presence*: The degree to which a brand feels omnipresent and is talked about positively by consumers, customers and opinion formers in both traditional and social media.

j) *Understanding*: The brand is not only recognized by customers, but there is also an in-depth knowledge and understanding of its distinctive qualities and characteristics. This would also include customer's understanding of the parent company.

5.3.4. Grow and sustain brand equity

Brands also need be managed over time. As noted above, one of the main reasons why brands fade and move from the leadership stage of the BAV into the eroding potential, is because the sources of their brand equity have not been protected enough over time.

The internal and external environments of a brand constantly change. Shifts in consumer behaviour, competition, regulation, other environmental factors and even internal factors (e.g., the strategic objectives) can affect the success of a brand. Therefore, effective brand management consists of proactive strategies aimed to maintain and enhance the brand equity over time.

Therefore, managers need to know how they can manage brands over time. They may wish to (1) extend the brand (i.e., use the same brand name in a different product category), they may need to (2) adjust the brand meaning or mix, and they may need to (3) revitalise the brand.

First, when considering a brand extension, there are two critical questions to be considered: First, how does a brand extension *leverage* the equity in the parent brand? And second, how effectively does the extension *contribute* to the equity in the parent brand? The advantages and disadvantages of brand extensions are depicted in Figure 48.

Figure 48. Advantages and disadvantages of brand extensions

Advantages	Disadvantages
▪ Reduce risk perceived by customers ▪ Permit consumer variety seeking ▪ Increase relevance of brand to new markets ▪ Increase probability of getting distribution and trial ▪ Increase efficiency of promotional expenditures ▪ Reduce costs of introducing and developing new brand ▪ Increase pricing breadth	▪ Confuse customers (weaker line logic) ▪ May lead to retailer resistance ▪ Failure can hurt parent brand's image ▪ Success can also hurt the parent brand's image (e.g., by diluting the original strong associations) ▪ Cannibalise parent brand's sales ▪ May weaken a brand's meaning ▪ Increased costs ▪ Opportunity cost of developing a new brand

Second, managers may need to reinforce their brand. The key consideration when managers are trying to reinforce their brand is the consistency of the amount and nature of the brand's marketing support. Brands with shrinking research and development and marketing communication budgets are at risk of becoming obsolete. Brands like Coca-Cola, BMW and others have been remarkably consistent in their strategies once they achieved a preeminent market leadership position. Consistency shouldn't mean avoiding making any changes. The tactics might change but the positioning of a brand can remain consistent over time.

Equally important to brand reinforcement is the need to protect a brand's sources of brand equity. Although brands should always look for potentially powerful new sources of brand equity, a top priority is to preserve and defend those sources of brand equity that already exist.

Marketers also face trade-offs between activities that fortify brand equity and those that capitalise on existing equity. Therefore, one should very carefully consider the activities that are designed to fortify vs leverage brand equity. Marketers can design marketing programmes that mainly try to capitalise on or maximise brand awareness and image (e.g., by reducing advertising expenses, seeking higher price premiums, introducing brand extensions). However, the more we rely on this strategy, the easier it is to neglect and perhaps diminish the brand and its source of equity.

Sometimes marketers may also need to fine-tune the supporting marketing programme, and change tactics when it is clear they no longer make the desired contribution to brand equity. This might involve changing product-related aspects or imagery associations.

Finally, the third option in growing and sustaining brand equity is brand revitalisation. The need to revitalise a brand is predominantly the result of neglect. Yet revitalisation should typically only be pursued where some values, favourability and awareness remain. The brand equity model suggests that there are two main ways to refresh old sources of brand equity: First, expand the depth or breadth of awareness. With a fading brand, often depth of awareness is not the problem, it is the breadth that can bring about some issues. That is, customers remember the brand but not at the right time and in the right context (e.g., when they should buy it). This issue may be addressed by identifying additional or new usage opportunities or identifying new and completely different ways to use the brand. Alternatively, brand managers can try to improve the strength and uniqueness of brand associations that build up the brand image, by repositioning the brand, finding points of parity with category leaders, establishing new points of difference or bringing the focus back on the old PoDs, and changing brand elements (e.g., name and logo).

6 STRATEGIC CUSTOMER RELATIONSHIP MANAGEMENT

Developing and nurturing relationships with valuable customers has become an important source of competitive advantage. Successful companies are becoming increasingly aware of the need to identify profitable customers and focus not just on individual transactions, but also on long-term relationships. There are two important questions that need attention: First, why is customer loyalty so important for business performance? What is the business case for building loyalty? And second, what exactly can a company do to build loyalty? We are going to discuss these two very important questions.

6.1 THE BUSINESS CASE FOR LOYALTY

There are two key factors that make the building of customer loyalty important: the growth and margins effects of loyalty.

The growth effect simply refers to the fact that if a company manages to retain more of its customers, its customer base grows over time, and hence it is able to retain more sources of revenue. A simple measure of loyalty is the Retention Rate (RR). A typical business may have an RR of 80%, which indicates that 80% of the customers that were served this year will return the following year (i.e., 20% of customers are lost). If a company were to increase its RR by a mere 5%, the first consequence of that increase would be that the customer base grows over time. Thus, the first effect of improving customer retention is a growth in the customer base and in the sources of revenue.

The second effect of loyalty, the margins effect, is something that is often neglected by organisations. In short, the margins effect refers to the fact that if the company increases customer retention, and hence the average time each customer stays with the company increases, not only does the company experience a growth in its customer base, but each individual customer also becomes more profitable on average. In other words, customers may be seen as assets of increasing value: the longer they stay with an organisation, the more profitable they become. There are at least six sources of customer profitability over time:

1. *Reduced acquisition costs*: obtaining new customers is expensive. In contrast, retaining an existing customer can be a lot cheaper.

Research has estimated that retaining a loyal customer is 4 to 7 times cheaper than attracting a new one.

2. *Base profit*: earnings on purchases before loyalty effects. This is the amount of money generated by sales of products that the customer initially sought from a seller. For example, assume that a customer signs up with Amazon.com to buy books. The sales of books to that customer over his or her relationship with Amazon constitute the base profit.

3. *Revenue growth*: loyal customers increase their spending over time, because of trust. Thus, a customer that has already purchased from Amazon.com may over time give more of his or her business (e.g., buy more books than initially planned, start making other purchases, such as DVDs and/or consumer products, from Amazon). In other words, trust and experience can generate more business over time, making a loyal customer increasingly more profitable.

4. *Operating costs*: A customer that is more familiar with the firm will generate a decrease in serving cost for the business. Initially, customers may require a lot of information and assistance. They might call the company repeatedly and use up customer service time, etc. On the other hand, a loyal customer is cheaper to serve, for example because he or she knows where to find product-related information, how to pay, how to use the products. In other words, the handholding often required to deal with new customers can be quite expensive and decreases over time as a customer transacts with the organisation.

5. *Referrals*: satisfied customers recommend the business to others. In other words, they may act as unpaid marketers for the firm. This effect can be quite powerful, as word of mouth is unbiased, and other potential new customers may pay more attention to the referrals than paid-for marketing communications. As customers stay with an organisation longer, they are more likely to make recommendations and help the business attract new customers.

6. *Price premiums*: old customers are often less price conscious than others. New customers are often attracted by bargains, special deals and low prices. Loyal customers are less likely to go back into the market every time they need a product that they have already been buying from a trusted source. The fact that they stop

comparing prices all the time means that they are more likely to become more price inelastic.

Figure 49 below illustrates these sources of customer profitability over time. It shows that if a firm increases the average length of time a customer purchases products from them, the average profitability of all customers also increases. This is the margins effect of customer loyalty.

Figure 49. Sources of customer profitability over time

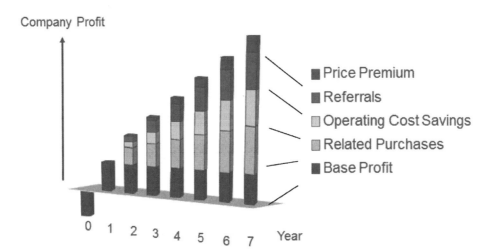

When we put together the growth and margins effects of loyalty, we can see how instrumental managing customer retention can be in improving a firm's profitability. Increasing the RR has the double effect of increasing a firm's customer base while also ensuring that each and every single one of the firm's customers becomes more profitable. Research has measured the effect of increasing loyalty, showing that in some cases, a mere increase in the RR of 5%, could increase business profitability by more than 80%. See figure 50 for further details.

As Figure 50 shows, in some industries, like financial services and insurance, an increase in customer retention can have a very significant impact on company profitability. It is unlikely that any other factor (particularly when considering the cost and effort involved) could have similar long-term effects.

Figure 50: Net profit impact of a 5% decrease in defection

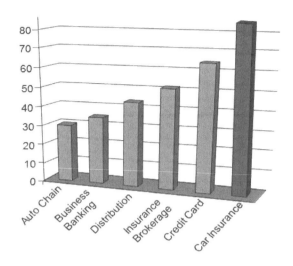

6.2 How to Build Loyalty

Given the importance of managing customer loyalty, it is surprising that some businesses still adopt a "leaky bucket approach" to customer management. Let us use the metaphor of a bucket to think of our customer base. The water in the bucket represents the customers we have. Some customers will evaporate out of the bucket. In other words, they will leave for completely acceptable reasons (e.g., they may move, die, etc.). However, other customers are leaking out of the bucket because the bucket has holes. These are customer defectors.

Obviously, a leaky bucket means that the water level (i.e., the size of our customer base) is dropping. A common way of dealing with this problem is to open the tap to refill the bucket. In other words, companies try to deal with the effect of customer defection by going back into the market and replacing lost customers with new ones. But hiding the effect of customer defection through new customer acquisition is possibly the most inefficient way to manage a company's customer base. This is because, as argued earlier, a customer that stays with a company for a long period of time is more profitable. Yet companies tend to ignore when such customers leave and happily replace them with new ones, often incurring very high acquisition costs. Remember: retaining an existing customer is a lot cheaper that attracting a new one. Instead of opening the tap, which can be very expensive and inefficient, a much better market strategy would be to fix the holes in the bucket first, so that when the tap is

173

opened, the size of the customer base actually increases, and the business grows.

So, what is the main source of holes in the firm's bucket? Research has shown that the biggest single hole is customer neglect. In other words, customers tend to leak out of a firm's bucket due to customer disregard, or the fact that customers are being sent clear signals that the company does not care about them or values them. Consequently, when customers feel neglected, they also feel free to shop around.

Figure 51: A leaky-bucket approach to customer management

The following are typical symptoms of customer disregard. They are the cues companies send to their customers that indicate that they do not care about them (and hence represent the main sources of "holes in the bucket"):

1. *Complicated complaint procedures*: making it difficult for customers to voice their concerns or to seek solutions to their problems is a sure sign that the company is transaction-oriented and does not want a relationship with its customers.

2. *Delays in product or service changes*: again, this is a clear sign that can destroy trust between an organisation and its customers. Remember that trust is a key driver of loyalty.

174

3. *Slow and grudging response to breakdowns*: when things go wrong, research has shown that customers do not care too much about what exactly is being done to rectify the problem, as much as they care about the fact that someone is working on the problem right away. When things go wrong, speed is a clear indicator that the company cares.

4. *Many escape clauses in promises & agreements*: while some legal jargon, terms and conditions are often unavoidable, too much of it can signal to customers that the firm is trying to absolve itself from any responsibility. This can be a clear sign of a sales instead of a market orientation.

5. *Premise that customers cause product/service problems*: blaming the customer for causing problems, often without any corroborating evidence, is a sure sign that the company does not see itself as the customer's partner and is not prepared to work towards dealing with arising issues. Another clear sign is when a firm is transaction and short-term orientated, instead of having a relational and long-term focus.

6. *Poor or non-existent customer-information management*: not knowing who a company's customers are, what they purchase, and their preferences is another clear sign of customer disregard. Nowadays, with the cost of information management constantly falling, there is no excuse for poor customer information and database management.

Addressing the issues above can be a very good starting point for organisations wishing to build customer loyalty by addressing the "holes in the bucket". There is another tactic that companies can use to build loyalty, and that is to create customer delight.

6.2.1. Customer delight as a key driver of loyalty

Going above and beyond merely satisfying consumers and creating "customer delight" is the sure way to create a customer base that is not only behaviourally loyal, but also attitudinally attached to the company or brand. Customer delight involves exceeding customer expectations and delivering a strong, positive and surprising experience to customers. Customer satisfaction is created when customers get what they want, for example because the product features meet their expectations. Customer delight, in contrast, is created when customers get something that they do not expect.

Customer delight may be created when companies focus not only on "satisfiers" but also on "attractive requirements". Product features that increase customer satisfaction beyond the basic product features are called satisfiers. High performance on a satisfier results in high customer satisfaction. Attractive requirements, on the other hand, are not explicitly expressed nor expected by the consumer, but are surprisingly enjoyable if met. If the attractive requirements are not met, there isn't necessarily a feeling of dissatisfaction. However, if they are met above and beyond the satisfiers, they can generate delight.

Figure 52: Customer satisfaction vs customer delight

	Customer Satisfaction	Customer Delight
Basis	Cognitive. Meeting or exceeding customer expectations	Affective. A mixture of joy and positive surprise that is beyond the customer's expectations
Result	The marketer has satisfied the contract with the customer	A more positive and more emotional response than simply excellent.
Key variables	Satisfiers	Attractive requirements
Word of mouth outcomes	Little reason to communicate their feelings. Weaker memory trace.	Delighted customers may become "apostles" of the brand. Delight is more memorable.
Appropriate management strategy	Recognise that meeting satisfier efforts may not be a sufficient competitive advantage.	Focus on attractive requirements after satisfiers are met.

The key difference between customer satisfaction and customer delight, then, is that while the former is a cognitive outcome (i.e., it is a rational response), the latter is more affective (i.e., it is more emotional in nature). It is exactly that difference that makes customer delight attractive to companies. After all, a customer that is merely satisfied because his or her expectations have been met, has very little reason to go out of his or her way to recommend the business to others and share his or her experience. On the other hand, as consumers we are more likely to recommend a business and share a positive experience when there is an element of positive surprise that comes with it. The challenge for organisations then is to engage both the minds and the hearts of their customers, as that can be a key driver of loyalty.

So how can customer delight be generated? The following are some interesting examples of ways in which companies can built customer delight by focusing not only on satisfiers, but also on attractive requirements:

- *Recognising the importance of courtesy, empathy, and efforts in understanding customer needs*
  - A study of 150 Indian executives who were asked to report a critical incident that was either delight or outrage, showed that how the customer was treated was the most important aspect of the service that contributed to service delight, with courtesy being the most cited factor. A recent US-based study in a retail setting (except grocery and drugstore) found "helpful", "friendly" and "willing to go outside the rules to help" as the top factors associated with delight.
  - A good example is Virgin Mobile. Virgin is known for a down-to-earth approach, and for not talking down to customers. It is often cited as an example of a company that has achieved success in a mature market (as a later entrant into the mobile market) by making the customer their partner and trying to understand exactly what they need.

- *Delivering unanticipated value*
  - This includes finding an unanticipated product, an unexpected bargain, or purchasing a product at a lower price than expected. As an example, this may be due to a firm's low-cost structure.
  - Jet Blue in the US airline industry is an appropriate example: its fares are not only 60% to 70% cheaper than other airlines' full economy fares, but Jet Blue also has new planes, leather seats, TV programming at every seat and live satellite programming. It ranks number 1 in the US in terms of customer satisfaction according to many reports.

- *Refusing to be content with merely satisfying consumers*
  - Firms need to think in terms of delight, not just satisfaction. This may be possible, for example, by using a firm's customer

database carefully and with a view to giving customers the unexpected.

- The hotel chain Ritz-Carlton is a good example: Its CEO and President was recently quoted saying that: "unless you have 100% customer satisfaction – and not just satisfaction, but true excitement about what you are doing – you can improve ... And if you do have 100% customer satisfaction, you have to make sure you listen just in case they change, so you can change with them". What sets Ritz-Carlton apart from other hotels is that in great hotels, if you want something you ask for it and it will be provided. At the Ritz-Carlton you don't have to ask. What enables this is their chain-wide guest-recognition database, to track all of the customers' preferences, from floor level, to food, newspaper, and even preferred beverage upon arrival.

- *Making sure that novelty and entertainment are provided*
  - In some industries, it is possible to provide some novelty and entertainment for customers, so that they are always surprised. This is about creating that "wow factor" that leaves a long-lasting and positive impression.
  - Clothes retailer Abercrombie & Fitch provides a good example: The brand reinvented itself from a store where an old gentleman would buy his gear for a weekend in the country, to a company with a new store concept. Stores feel like a mix between a fashion show, a dance party and a cool place for cool people to hang out. This is achieved, for example, through sophisticated lighting, loud and trendy music, male and female models posing for pictures with customers.

- *Focusing on multiple points of contact with the customer*
  - This is not just about producing a "new and improved" product all the time. Companies also need to focus on the setting where customers buy their product, the delivery system, and the service function that resolves service issues.
  - The airline SAS is a good case in point: Its CEO Jan Carlzon coined the phrase "moment of truth" to refer to the multiple contacts a customer has with an organisation. According to Carlzon, any contact can make or break the organisation. A company that wants to delight has to focus on every point of contact with the customer.

178

- *Repositioning the business to deliver solutions as opposed to products and services*
  - Managers need to focus on outcomes, rather than products, and on the value that is delivered to customers. They can start by asking the questions: What are customers really buying? What is the ultimate benefit which they seek from the market? How can we go above expectations in delivering those benefits?
  - The French B2B company Chauffagistes is a good example: the company pioneered a new concept in heating and cooling. Instead of selling products like heaters and air conditioning, the firm promises to maintain a certain amount of floor space at an agreed temperature.

In summary, what are some potential sources of customer delight over customer satisfaction? In a satisfactory experience, value, variety service, and so on are all within the buyer's expectation set. These things are positive but fit within the buyer's existing expectations. In contrast, delightful experiences are outside the buyer's existing expectation set. These are things that most customers would not expect. Therefore, a good starting point to develop customer delight is to, first, identify areas of performance where consumer expectations do not exist. Then, start thinking outside the box!

6.2.2. Customer engagement

The discussion above suggests that the link between customer satisfaction and loyalty is not a straight-forward one. Most customers are apathetic towards brands, so much so that even when they are satisfied, they will not be loyal. Indeed, evidence suggests that often even highly satisfied customers leave. One way of dealing with this challenge is to aim for customer delight, as discussed in the previous section. Another is to leverage the missing links between customer satisfaction and loyalty. In other words: if customer satisfaction is not enough to drive repeat business, is there anything else above and beyond customer satisfaction that can make customers more loyal therefore more profitable for the firm? What are the missing links in the relationship between customer satisfaction and repeat purchase?

Word of Mouth and the Net Promoter Score

Marketing scholars have heralded positive word of mouth (WOM) as one of the missing links between satisfaction and purchase behaviour. In other words, customers who are very satisfied, and who will actively go out of their way to recommend a business to other customers, are more likely to repurchase and tend to be more profitable. Because WOM is perceived to be less biased and more trustworthy than information from traditional marketing campaigns, it is considered a strong determinant of customer buying behaviour and new customer acquisition. Furthermore, because individuals put their own reputation on the line when recommending a firm to others, willingness to provide positive WOM indicates a strong relationship between firms and their customers.

This phenomenon led marketing researcher Reichheld to develop the Net Promoter Score (NPS), which is a marketing metric designed as an alternative to traditional customer satisfaction surveys. The NPS is being used by most Fortune 1000 companies, primarily because of its simplicity (it involves asking just one question), its impact on responses (it can lead to a higher response rate and responses from more profitable customers who may not be inclined to complete lengthy surveys), and its predictive power (it has been shown to correlate with revenue growth).

To calculate the NPS, a firm only has to ask the customer one single question: "How likely is it that you would recommend our company/product/service to a friend or colleague?" on a 0 to 10 scale. Customers who score a 9 or 10 are called Promoters, and they usually express more value-creating behaviours: they buy more, make positive referrals to potential customers and remain with the firm longer. Those who respond with a score of 0 to 6 are called Detractors, and they are believed to be less likely to exhibit the value-creating behaviours. Responses of 7 and 8 are considered to be Passives, and their behaviour falls between Promoters and Detractors.

To calculate the NPS, one has to subtract the percentage of "detractor" customers from the percentage of "promoter" customers. Therefore, an NPS can be as low as –100 (every respondent is a "detractor") or as high as +100 (every respondent is a "promoter"). Just as net worth represents the difference between financial assets and liabilities, the NPS quantifies the difference between customer assets and liabilities. A growth engine running at perfect efficiency would convert 100% of a company's customers into promoters. The worst possible engine would convert 100% into detractors. The best way to measure the efficiency of the growth engine is to take the percentage of customers who are promoters (P) and subtract the percentage who are detractors (D).

NPS scores vary across different industries, but a positive NPS (i.e., one that is higher than zero) is generally deemed good, an NPS above 50% is generally deemed excellent, and anything over 70% is exceptional. Perhaps more interesting than absolute numbers, however, is an examination of the trend. That is, an improvement in the NPS is a sign that the relationship between the firm and its customers is getting stronger. A declining NPS should be a source of concern.

Firms could also follow the NPS question with an open-ended question asking customers to elaborate the reasons for their rating of the firm or the product. The answers gained through the open-ended questions can be shared with front-line employees and management to facilitate follow-up actions and change. However, the NPS question should never appear alongside other questions, or the benefit of simplicity is lost. It may also be interesting to find out what the priorities of promoters are, what their profile is, as these can be the most profitable customers. Knowing their characteristics may allow us to design a strategy to acquire more of them.

What does the NPS tell us? Companies with high NPSs earn growth rather than "buy" it. This measure demonstrates that two conditions must be satisfied before customers make a personal referral: They must believe that the company offers superior value (thus engaging their rational side), and they must feel good about their relationship with the company (thus engaging their emotional side as well).

The average lifetime value of promoters is three to eight times that of detractors, depending on the industry or market segment. Promoters stay longer with the company, buy more products, usually cost less to serve and are more likely to refer the supplier to other customers. B2B research shows that NPS correlates closely with sales growth, expanded share of wallet, sales force productivity, greater market share, greater employee engagement and higher profitability. As a result, both B2B loyalty leaders, for example, tend to grow four to eight percentage points above their market's annual growth.

Customer participation

Because WOM involves customer-to-customer interaction, it may be seen as an "external" type of customer activity. Yet, there is plenty of evidence suggesting that a more internally oriented activity, i.e., customer-to-firm interaction, may also be crucial: marketers have been told for years that customer feedback, suggestions and input regarding product and service improvements are key to customer retention. Whilst satisfied customers may still tend to defect, actively encouraging their participation, could be instrumental in fostering repeat business. In some cases, companies can recapture more than a third of defectors merely by contacting them and encouraging their feedback. Clearly, a mechanism other than WOM that ensures that a satisfied customer buys more of a company's products and services is customer participation.

Customer participation involves customers providing businesses with suggestions, feedback and ideas about the company's products and services. Participation can benefit organisations in several ways. Whether this happens through surveys, comment cards, compliment/complaint forms, online feedback forms or other means, the advantages of treating customers as consultants are well documented. Encouraging customer participation can create a bond between customers and the organisation that increases customer loyalty and even propensity to pay. Consequently, managers should try to embrace customer participation and relax the assumption that insiders always know best.

So how can customer participation be encouraged and managed? The following six strategies can help a company implement customer participation programs effectively:

1. *Don't be afraid of participation*

    Managers may fear that if they pay too much attention to customers' feedback, their business can lose its focus. On the contrary, research has established that firms that seek out and implement feedback gained from customers have more profitable relationships with them and possess a more engaged customer base who appreciate the company and are grateful that the company values their feedback.

2. *Start simple and expand over time*

    Managers may feel that seeking out and implementing customer feedback is overwhelming and complex. Quite the opposite, the easier it is for the customer to share their feedback, the more likely one is to do so, and stay engaged. After the first initial step in gathering customer feedback is established, the company can roll out a more complex, sophisticated platform to generate insights. For instance, Apple gathers customer feedback from various sources: Apple Support Communities, forums, Express Lane advanced support website, online communities such as Apple Customer Pulse or measuring WOM in-store and online.

182

3. *Move from the tactical to the strategic*

Even though some companies have implemented the insights gained from customer participation programs, some have failed to harness all the benefits arising from them. Customer feedback can start off as a tactical change within the business but should progress into being a more strategic initiative.

4. *Let customer participation and social media support one another*

Customer participation can be bolstered through integrating it with the organisation's social media support system. For instance, an airline could use the feedback a customer shares on social media and communicate it with the cabin crew onboard the flight. This way, the airline can address a potential problem in real time and increase customer satisfaction.

5. *Make customers feel like they're in control*

Customers prefer to feel that their participation is voluntary, rather than controlled by the firm. Customers do not like to be bombarded by feedback requests and often lose trust in the company as a consequence. An effective strategy for the firm could be to set up a Facebook community to gather feedback and foster voluntary participation.

6. *Be creative about how you manage participation*

When customers participate and invest their time to provide feedback, they do so with the hope that their time will not be wasted, and their feedback will be addressed. If a customer feels that their ideas are ignored, they will be unlikely to participate. Companies can make sure that customers know that their feedback is valued, for instance, by sharing how the feedback would be used in shaping firm policies.

As highlighted above, fostering customer feedback and insights is a powerful tool to build a satisfied customer base that could become loyal, buy more of the company's products and generate more profits for the business. Consequently, companies should strive to foster both WOM and customer participation at the same time, as research findings suggest that customers who engage in both activities are the most profitable ones.

However, implementation of customer participation is not without risks. Senior executives may extol the virtues of turning customers into consultants, but frontline employees (FLEs), for example, often appear less eager. In fact, when customers are encouraged to speak up, the relationship between frontline employees and the company may be tested. Customer participation may require employees to relay information not in employees' own interest (e.g., customer complaints, suggestions that may add to employees' workload, sources of unwanted changes, etc.). And when it influences their career and job security, it can disempower employees and drive detachment. Reliance on customer participation may also lead employees to become overly tolerant of poor customer behaviour, such as verbal and physical abuse, for their own survival, which can lead to negative emotional and behavioural consequences. Feelings of betrayal and frustration can ensue when a company appears to value customer-generated information more than that of its employees. This can quickly change employees' initially positive attitude towards the business into indifference, numbness or even resentment.

Thus, while customer participation can be beneficial, if managers do not get it right, FLEs are not only less likely to support it, they may also go so far as to actively sabotage it. Furthermore, employee sabotage is the fastest way to kill any business. There are several ways in which businesses can overcome this dark side of customer participation, to keep employees engaged and believe that management has their backs, whilst at the same time reaping the rewards of customer participation.

1. *Don't overemphasize customer feedback in performance evaluations*

   Customers sometimes evaluate employees based on subjective factors that the employee has no control over (e.g. long waiting times). Using such feedback from customers to evaluate employee performance may be counterproductive, as it can weaken employees' motivation to serve the customer. Therefore, it is better not to overemphasize customer feedback in the performance evaluation of employees.

2. *Foster a culture of respect for front-line employees*

   You may have experienced a front-line employee asking you for a good feedback on a follow-up survey. Firms need to create a culture where front-line employees are not compelled to beg customers for scores and engage in opportunistic or even manipulative behaviour. A company that effectively built a culture of putting employees and not customers first is Southwest Airlines. Consequently, many of its employees are willing to go the extra mile to ensure customer satisfaction.

3. *Make employee well-being a real priority*

Respecting, but also understanding front-line employees' wellbeing is key for success. Companies can introduce employee service counters to support workers who experienced a negative interaction with the customer in the form of incidents such as harassment, stalking or verbal assault. For instance, 3M organizes employee retreats where their workers can share their negative experiences with each other, hence helping them re-establish a sense of equilibrium.

4. *Confirm that the customer is not always king*

Research has shown that employees often fear of speaking out in case of unacceptable customer requests or bad treatment. Front-line employees often lose the positive feelings of work due to the behaviour of some ill-mannered customers. A good example of a company that managed to put the employees' well-being first is Hyundai Card: the credit card company allows its employees at call centres to terminate a call when the customer is being unreasonable or abusive.

5. *Treat external and internal participation as equally important*

Even though managing customer participation can pose some challenges to employees and management, a company can still benefit from customer feedback as argued above. However, a balanced approach of merging customer satisfaction and participation with employee well-being is needed. A company that successfully fosters such approach is WestJet: when the company was considering starting a regional airline, WestJet did not only ask customers about their opinions, but also consulted employees. This made sure employees felt valued, while the company benefitted from receiving key information from all stakeholders.

6.2.3. The Problem with CRM

Because of the enormous potential benefits of managing one's customer base strategically, Customer Relationship Management (CRM) has captured the imagination of many managers. CRM software spending is in excess of $50 billion in the USA alone. With its emphasis on identifying valuable customers, securing their loyalty through tailor-made offerings, and reducing costs of serving them, CRM has seized managers' imaginations. So why do 55% of CRM projects, according to a recent study, drive customers away and actually dilute earnings? The answer: Because CRM is erroneously seen as a software that manages customer relationships for you. However, it is not. CRM is about bundling customer-focused strategy and processes to boost customer loyalty and profitability. Technology simply supports that strategy.

Strictly speaking, CRM is about gathering customer data, identifying the most valuable customers over time, and increasing customer loyalty by offering superior value. This does not have to be a sophisticated or a high-tech process. Yet, many companies still get CRM wrong. There are at least four key reasons why CRM projects fail:

- *Implementing CRM before creating a customer strategy*

  First you need to create a customer acquisition and retention strategy, before you invest into a CRM technology. The first step is to segment customers based on how profitable they are for your business, then decide which relationships to invest into, how to increase margins and manage your costs, and divest consumers who do not bring in profits. Then you can ask strategic questions such as: "How much time and money can we allocate to CRM? How can we build relationships now—without spending on technology?"

  For example, facing flattening circulation, the New York Times refined its customer strategy. It identified potential subscribers in cities across the nation, pinpointed their needs (e.g., earlier home delivery), then met those needs. The needs were met, for example, by upgrading its distribution capabilities with networked print sites. A decade before installing CRM technology, its circulation rose 2% and its customer-retention rate hit 94%. The retention rate is considered very high in an industry that averages a retention rate of 60%.

186

- *Rolling out CRM before changing the organisation to match*

To avoid this most dangerous pitfall, take time before a CRM rollout to make the organisation customer focused. In order to meet customer needs, you may need to reconfigure your existing processes (e.g. job descriptions, compensation systems, performance measures). This can take years. 87% of CRM failures stem from insufficient change management!

For example, to meet its sales goals, industrial equipment maker Square D had to focus on customers as never before. The company decided to overhaul some key systems (e.g., base the incentive strategy on the number of acquired customers) and reorganise its SBUs around four markets (e.g., residential, industrial). As a result of these changes, the company has seen an investment of $75MM in a high-tech order-management system, just three years after the launch of the above-described initiative.

- *Assuming that more CRM technology is better*

Some companies fulfil their CRM objectives with low-tech approaches, then phase in higher-tech solutions.

For instance, Grand Expeditions, a tour management company was able to map out some low-tech activities that helped to enhance its relationship with customers (e.g., thank-you notes sent to clients after the excursions by the tour operators). Only after replicating these activities across the company did Grand Expeditions evaluate CRM software and more high-tech solutions.

- *Stalking, not wooing customers*

CRM always starts with identifying the right customers: those who want a relationship with you. Then you should contact them in ways they value. Remember: Just because you can contact customers does not mean you should!

For example, when its telemarketing program began annoying customers and decreasing circulation, the Dallas Morning News built "wantedness". It launched a direct-mail campaign targeting customers prequalified for growth potential and emphasized retention by calling customers only to check satisfaction and offer automated payments. The telemarketing retention rates were 40%, whereas the direct-mail retention rates increased to 62%.

6.2.4. Brand transparency

Brand transparency can be a powerful weapon in a company's strategic arsenal. Forward-thinking managers in a wide range of industries harness the benefits of providing accessible and objective information to their current and potential customers. These benefits include a reduction in customers' price sensitivity, through the trust that it engenders in customers, as well as increased loyalty.

Transparency involves making objective and candid brand-related information available to customers, for example, by encouraging them to publish comments and reviews on the company website, comparing the company's products and services to those of the competition in an objective and unbiased fashion, publishing genuine benchmark data even when it is not completely favourable, and so on. Evidence suggests that customers will pay more and will become more loyal when dealing with a transparent brand.

Transparency entails, first, providing information that is easily understood by the target audience. When too much or too complex information is provided to customers, transparency may backfire as customers face even higher levels of uncertainty, which may result in negative reactions or alienation. Second, the information that is shared also needs to be objective. It cannot selectively exaggerate positive attributes and discount negatives ones. Hence, a strong transparency strategy should embody truth and honesty.

There are several transparency strategies that companies can follow, and they are summarised in Figure 53.

Figure 53: The seven strategies of transparency

Strategy	Description	Examples
Balance quality and quantity of information	<ul><li>It is important for the firm to manage the direct flow of information, its quantity and quality</li><li>Too much information can signal that the company is not aware what is important for the customer</li></ul>	<ul><li>A good example is an airline that has a specific review section solely for business travellers</li></ul>

	- Information provided to customers should also be useful, relevant and easily comprehensible, help reduce uncertainty and induce trust - Managers should also study whether a set of information is relevant for the whole customer base or just certain segments, and hence disseminate information accordingly through the most appropriate social media channels - Visually appealing images can also help transparency initiatives	- Lush Fresh Handmade Cosmetics uses enticing and colourful pictures to communicate its brand message and identity with customers
Make sure that the information is part of customer's purchasing process and they receive it at the right time	- With the myriad of information available online, there is a risk that consumers will be unable to find critically relevant information about the business - The quantity, type, nature of information, as well as when and how customers receive it is as important as the quality of information - Companies can address this by well-designed user experiences and service experience strategies and tactics	- SugarSync, an online backup and file-sharing platform, provides customers with a benchmark tool on their website, to help consumers compare competitor offerings and highlight that SugarSync is a better alternative - Transferwise.com provides an online calculator to provide customers with an accurate estimate of their savings when using their services
Help your customers help you	- Your customers can be crucial resources in obtaining performance transparency. A business can use customer reviews, ratings or feedback to signal to other customers that the information the company discloses is objective - Knowing what the customers prefer and what needs to be improved through the feedback received from consumers is useful to identify. These insights can drive the nature of the information that is shared by the company on different channels	- A company CEO in the paper and pulp industry argued that knowing why consumers leave to competitors does not only help to improve the company's offering, but also the information shared to customers that enhances transparency - McDonald's "Our Food. Your Questions" campaign did not only increase the organisation's transparency efforts but helped to gather feedback on

		what bothers customers and what they seek to have improved • Adidas collects customer feedback on the Adidas Boost running shoe line through customers sharing their experiences with one another
Managing transparency is both a proactive and a reactive process	• Companies that successfully exploit transparency adopt a both proactive and reactive structure • These companies would be deemed proactive as they seek out information relevant to customers, but they would also be thought of as reactive in terms of monitoring and responding to customer reviews	• When Tesla was subject of damaging reviews in 2013, Tesla's CEO Elon Musk responded to the reviews with a blog post releasing actual logged vehicle data addressing the review. The media appraised the move by highlighting that reacting fast and in a transparent fashion was a good strategy to follow
Embrace transparency even if it means negative reviews	• Transparency could be used by firms that lack a strong reputation as a means to increase customer purchase intention and willingness to pay • Transparency can act as a differentiating strategy • Reading negative information about the firm builds customers' confidence as it makes customers more aware of the pros and cons of the business, and make them feel as they are more informed and less concerned about potential risks • Negative feedback can help establish trust, as it can show customers that the firm is able to handle the situation, and the firm actually cares about the customers, as well as its own products or services • As customers can share their negative feedback through various channels, it is the best strategy for the firm to encourage sharing these feedbacks on platforms that are monitored by the firm	• The CEO of a fast-growing online service company said that: "sharing the good and the bad makes us more like our customers. They are not selective in the information they share. So why should we?"

Transparency is more than just customer-generated reviews	• Transparency can also be implemented through: 1. Communicating to customers what the firm thinks is important about the business relative to the competition. This helps customers understand the value offered by the firm 2. Being honest about the risks and costs associated with dealing with the firm (e.g. switching costs, time, effort) 3. Showing the difficulties in meeting customers' needs with the aim of setting appropriate customer expectations	• Zappos's employees help customers search for competitors' products that Zappos does not sell • EDF Energy regularly benchmarks its prices against competitors and sends this information to the customers • The UK TV show "Airline" that follows the workers of EasyJet helps consumers understand the complex world of airline operations by humanising the context and setting appropriate expectations • IKEA is transparent about the durability of its furniture and sets customers' expectations through its "commitment-free approach to furniture buying."
Utilise neutral third-party websites	• Customers do not only gather company information through a firm's own website, but also through third-party websites, such as: • Horizontal third-party review sites that aggregate customer reviews (e.g. Trustpilot.com) • Vertical third-party review sites that aggregate business offerings (e.g. booking.com, TripAdvisor) • Social media platforms that enable the sharing of user-generated content and reviews (e.g. Facebook, Twitter, LinkedIn, Instagram) • A company can either aggregate the reviews from third party sites to their own website, or alternatively make the website information available on third party sites	• Feefo makes it possible for businesses to gather customer reviews on the firm's own website, and then through transferring these to Feefo's aggregation website, submitting them to Google as reviews and to social media as ratings. Such service is highly valued by the firms, as their click-through rate and conversion increases, along with enabling the collection of relevant customer information in a cost-effective manner

PART III: SOURCES, REFERENCES AND FURTHER READINGS

Aaker, D.A. (1996) "Measuring brand equity across products and markets", California Management Review, 38(3): pp.102-120.

Barwise, P. & Meehan, S. (2004) "Simply Better: Winning and Keeping Customers by Delivering What Matters Most", Boston: Harvard Business School Publishing Corporation.

BAV group (2020) "BrandAsset Valuator" https://www.bavgroup.com/about-bav/brandassetr-valuator

Blattberg, R.C., Getz, G. & Thomas, J.S. (2001) "Managing Customer Retention" in Customer equity: building and managing relationships as valuable assets. Boston, Mass.: Harvard Business School Press.

Borden, N.H. (1984) "The Concept of the Marketing Mix", Journal of Adverting Research, II: pp. 1-12.

Day, G.S. (1981) "The product life cycle: analysis and applications issues", Journal of Marketing, 45(4): pp.60-67.

Dixon, M., Freeman, K & Toman, N. (2010) "Stop Trying to Delight Your Customers", Harvard Business Review, 88(7), pp: 1-7.

Dube, J.P. & Misra, S. (2019) "Personalized Pricing and Customer Welfare", Chicago Booth School of Business Working Paper.

Ehrenberg, A (1974) "Repetitive advertising and the consumer" Journal of Advertising Research, 14: pp. 25-34.

Ehrenberg, A (1988) "Repeat-buying: facts, theory and applications", 2nd ed., Edward Arnold, London; Oxford University Press, New York.

Eisingerich, A.B., Auh, S. & Merlo, O. "Acta Non Verba? The Role of Customer Participation and Word of Mouth in the Relationship Between Service Firms' Customer Satisfaction and Sales Performance", Journal of Service Research 17(1), pp: 40-53.

Gaski, J.F. (1984) "The theory of power and conflict in channels of distribution", Journal of Marketing, 48(3): pp.9-29.

Griffin, J. (2002) "Customer loyalty: how to earn it, how to keep it", San Francisco: Jossey-Bass.

Interbrand (2020) "Interbrand's Best Global Brands" https://www.inter-brand.com/best-brands/best-global-brands/2019/download/

Jones, T.O. & Sasser, W.E. (1995) "Why Satisfied Customers Defect", Harvard Business Review, 73, pp. 88-99.

Keller, K.L. (1993) "Conceptualizing, measuring, and managing customer-based brand equity", Journal of Marketing, 57(January), 1-22.

Keller, K.L. (2012) "Strategic Brand Management: Building, Measuring, and Managing Brand Equity. Global Edition", 4th ed., Harlow: Pearson Education Limited.

Kim, J. & Morris, J.D. (2003) "The effect of advertising on the market value of firms: empirical evidence from the Super Bowl ads", Journal of Targeting, Measurement & Analysis for Marketing, 12(1): pp.53-65.

Kliatchko, J. (2005) "Towards a new definition of Integrated Marketing Communications (IMC)", International Journal of Advertising, 24(1): pp.7-34.

Kotler, P. (1999) "Kotler on Marketing" New York: The Free Press.

Layton, R.A. (2007). Marketing Systems- A Core Macromarketing Concept. Journal of Macromarketing, 27(3): pp. 227-242.

Lindemann, J. (2010) The Brand Value Chain. In: The Economy of Brands. London: Palgrave Macmillan.

Macrotrends (2019) "Coca-Cola Market Cap 2006-2019" https://www.macrotrends.net/stocks/charts/KO/coca-cola/market-cap

Mark, M. & Pearon, C. (2001) "The Hero and the Outlaw: building extraordinary brands through the power of archetypes", New York: McGraw-Hill.

McPhillips, S. and Merlo, O. (2008) Media convergence and the evolving media business model: An overview and strategic opportunities, The Marketing Review, 8(3): pp.237-253.

Merlo, O., Eisingerich, A.B. & Auh, S. (2014) "Why Customer Participation Matters" MIT Sloan Management Review, 55(2), pp:81-88.

Merlo, O., Eisingerich, A.B., Shin, H. & Britton, R.A. (2019) "Avoiding the Pitfalls of Customer Participation", MIT Sloan Management Review, 61(1), pp: 10-12.

Merlo, O. Eisingerich, A.B. Auh, S. & Levstek, J. (2018) "The benefits and implementation of performance transparency: The why and how of letting your customers 'see through' your business", Business Horizons, 61(1): pp.73-84.

Mohr, J. & Nevin, J.R. (1990) "Communication strategies in marketing channels: a theoretical perspective", Journal of Marketing, 54(4): pp.36-51.

Ofcom (2018) "Communications Market Report" UK Communications Market Report 2018. https://www.ofcom.org.uk/__data/assets/pdf_file/0022/117256/CMR-2018-narrative-report.pdf

Oliver, R.L. (1999) "Whence customer loyalty?", Journal of Marketing, 63(4): pp.33-44.

Rao, V.R. (1984) "Pricing research in marketing: the state of the art", Journal of Business, 57(1): pp.39-60.

Reichheld, F.F. (2003) "The One Number You Need to Grow" Harvard Business Review, 81(12), pp: 46-54.

Reichheld, F.F., Schefter, P. & Rigby D.K. (2002) "Avoid the Four Perils of CRM", Harvard Business Review, February 2002 Issue.

Robicheaux, R.A. & El-Ansary, A.I. (1976/77) "A general model for understanding channel member behaviour", Journal of Retailing, 52(4): pp.13-30, 93-94.

Rogers, E.M. (1983) "Diffusion of Innovations" 3rd edition. London: The Free Press.

Rust, R.T., Thompson, D.V. & Hamilton, R. (2006) Defeating Feature Fatigue, Harvard Business Review, February.

Sharp, B. (2010) How brands grow: What marketers don't know. Oxford: Oxford University Press.

Schlegelmilch, B.B. (2016) "Global Supply Chains and Distribution Networks" In: Global Marketing Strategy. Management for Professionals. Cham: Springer.

Sheth, J.N. & Parvatiyar, A. (1995) "The evolution of relationship marketing", International Business Review, 4(4): pp.397-418.

Spenner, P. & Freeman, K. (2012) "To keep your customers, keep it simple", Harvard Business Review, May.

Tellis, G.J. (1986) "Beyond the many faces of price: an integration of pricing strategies", Journal of Marketing, 50(4): pp.146-160.

Vargo, S.L. & Lusch, R.F. (2004) "Evolving to a new dominant logic for marketing", Journal of Marketing, 68(1): pp.1-17.

Whitwell, G., Lukas, B. & Doyle, P. (2003) Marketing Management: A Strategic Value-Based Approach", Milton, Australia: John Wiley & Sons.

Zeithaml, V.A., Parasuraman, A. & Berry, L.L. (1985) "Problems and strategies in services marketing", Journal of Marketing, 49(2): pp.33-46.

Published by Amazon (London, United Kingdom)

ISBN: 9798625632492

Printed in Great Britain
by Amazon

26885979R00112